# Milestones

## Rites of Passage in a Multi-Faith Community

## Celia Collinson and Campbell Miller

Photographs by Nick Hedges and David Richardson
John Twinning, Juliette Soester and Jan Siegeda

**Hodder & Stoughton**

LONDON SYDNEY AUCKLAND

*British Library Cataloguing in Publication Data*
Collinson, Celia
  Milestones
  1. Religious education
  I. Title    II. Miller, Campbell
  200'.7'1242    LC410.G7

  ISBN 0 7131 09610

First published 1984
Impression number 19 18 17 16 15 14 13 12 11 10
Year                    1998 1997 1996 1995 1994 1993

Printed in Great Britain for Hodder & Stoughton Educational,
a division of Hodder Headline PLC,
Mill Road, Dunton Green,
Sevenoaks, Kent TN13 2YA by The Bath Press, Avon.

# Preface

The primary concern of Religious Education is not with the passing on to pupils of a body of religious knowledge – facts and information about religious practices and ideas; Religious Education is much more concerned with stimulating thought about questions of meaning, purpose and values, and exploring areas of life and human experience which have a certain air of mystery about them and which are regarded by many as having the deepest significance.

A study of ceremonies concerned with the important life events – birth, initiation (or ceremonies of commitment as we prefer to call them), marriage and death, provides a particularly important avenue for such exploration.

Since it is a fact that in virtually all human societies there is a religious ceremony for these major life events (and even in non-religious societies such events as marriage and death are marked with a ceremony), it is clear that such events have a place of unique significance.

In portraying ceremonies of birth, commitment, marriage and death, we have of course presented facts and information; we have attempted to do this, however, in such a way that questions of meaning, purpose and values have been raised. We have tried especially to do this through the pupil *tasks* which we hope offer scope for activity by pupils of varying abilities. It is also our hope that the photographs not only support the information but also contribute towards an insight into the significance of such events in the lives of committed individuals.

We would emphasise, as we did in our earlier book, *Believers*, that we have set out to portray ceremonies *as we have found them* being practised within religious communities representative of the five major faiths which are followed in the multi-faith Britain of today.

It is our hope that pupils who use this book will come away from their study not merely with some knowledge of the ceremonies observed in the five faiths, but especially with insights into the significance of religion. We hope also that it will have prompted questions about meaning and purpose which are raised by the major life events of birth, marriage and death, and developed an awareness of the challenge to commitment which is an essential feature of man's religious quest.

# Acknowledgements

The authors wish to record their gratitude to the following: members of the various religious communities for their willingness to talk to them and help them in their understanding of the different ways in which important religious ceremonies are observed. They are especially grateful to those who were prepared to allow photographs to be taken of these ceremonies even when, in many cases, they were intimate family occasions; Mrs Ivy Gutridge, Secretary of Wolverhampton Inter-Faith Group, for advice and assistance with contacts within the various faith communities; Nick Hedges, David Richardson, John Twinning, Juliette Soester and Jan Siegeda for their willingness to provide the photographs which form an important part of this book.

The publishers would like to thank the following for their permission to reproduce copyright photographs:

Keystone Press: p 61;

Nick Hedges: pp 9, 10, 11t & b, 18, 21, 42, 43, 49, 50, 51t & b, 52, 53tl & b, 55, 67, 68, 69, 97t & b, 98, 99, 100, 101, 102, 108, 110t & b, 111l;

Juliette Soester: pp 12, 14, 15, 16, 17, 46;

John Twinning: pp 22, 23, 24, 38, 40, 64, 66, 71, 72, 73, 74t & b, 75, 76;

David Richardson: pp 25, 26, 28t & b, 29, 31, 32, 33, 34, 35, 45tr, 47, 53tr, 56, 59t & b, 62, 77, 78, 79t & b, 80b, 81, 82, 84, 86t & b, 87, 88, 89, 90, 91, 92t & b, 93, 111r, 119t & b, 120, 122, 123, 124;

Jan Siegeda: pp 113, 115, 116.

The publishers also wish to thank the following for permission to include copyright material:

Collins Liturgical Publications for Psalm 23 from the Liturgical Psalter in ASB © English text 1976, 1977, David L Frost, John A Emerton, Andrew A Macintosh, All rights reserved; The General Synod of the Church of England for extracts from alternative services in The Alternative Service Book 1980 are ©the Central Board of Finance of the Church of England are reproduced with permission; Routledge and Kegan Paul plc for Gandhi's horoscope from M E Jones: *How to Learn Astrology,* horoscope by George McCormack of Astrotech and Singer's Prayer-Book Publication Committee for extracts from the Authorised Daily Prayer Book. Bible passages are from the Revised Standard Version of the Bible published by the National Council of the Churches of Christ, the Jerusalem Bible published by Darton, Longman and Todd Ltd and the Good News Bible published by The British and Foreign Bible Society.

# Contents

# Introduction

Milestones mark stages in a journey: they also serve as guides, in the sense that they indicate that you are still following the road on which you set out.

Life is often regarded as a journey, and there are many milestones, the most important of which are probably birth, marriage and death.

Every religion regards these as events of great significance and marks them with ceremonies, some simple, others quite complex.

This book sets out to help you explore such ceremonies relating to birth, commitment, marriage and death in five of the major religions which are practised in Britain today – Hinduism, Judaism, Christianity, Islam and Sikhism. Such ceremonies are often referred to as 'Rites of Passage'.

Birth, marriage and death are the experiences in life which especially raise questions about the meaning and purpose of our existence on earth; probably this is one reason why, for centuries, man has felt it necessary to mark these important events with a ceremony. This is one of the ways in which he pursues his search for meaning, which brings purpose and enrichment into life.

Many people discover that their search for meaning and purpose is assisted by the beliefs and way of life offered by a particular religious faith and therefore commit themselves to that faith, its basic beliefs and the way of life which follows from these beliefs. There is often a ceremony to mark such a decision to commit themselves to the faith and that becomes another significant milestone in their lives.

In following the course offered by this book, you will learn certain facts about the various faiths and their ceremonies. More importantly, however, you will be given the opportunity to think more deeply about why people have such ceremonies, why these events are so significant, and what you believe yourself about the areas of life with which they are concerned.

# Part I

# Birth Ceremonies

# 1

# Hindu

The birth of a child in a Hindu family is a happy event, just as it is for most people around the world. In India, the country where most Hindus are to be found, it is often the custom in villages, when news of a birth is announced, to chant a song to express the joy which such news brings:

'From where are the sounds of happiness O friends, the sound comes from some happy mother's home.
From one place, greetings are being sent; At the other, a darling has just been born.'

The birth of a child begins a series of ceremonies which will occur at various stages during the life of a Hindu. These ceremonies are known as **Samskaras,** which means 'sacred rituals or acts'. They are important because they are believed to mark the significant developments in life. In a sense, each ceremony indicates the movement from one stage of life to another and each is therefore accompanied by prayers and readings from Hindu scriptures.

## At Birth

One of the Samskaras which occurs very soon after birth is that in which the baby is carefully washed in a ceremonial way and the shape of the word **Aum** is made with honey on the baby's tongue. **Aum** or **Om** is the way by which Hindus refer to God.

## The Naming Ceremony

We shall see that virtually every religion has a ceremony at which a baby is named. In Hinduism, prior to this naming ceremony, a priest has usually prepared a horoscope for the child in which he has taken account of such factors as the time and date of birth, the place of birth, the relative position of stars and planets at the time, and the parents' names. He will also have suggested several names which he considers suitable and usually the parents will have chosen the name from these.

On page 9 is a horoscope for Mahatma Gandhi who was a very famous Hindu.

A baby was born to the Patel family and they followed the custom by having the naming ceremony in their home eleven days after the birth of their baby son. Members of the family and friends gathered for this happy occasion at which prayers were said and then the priest announced that the name chosen for the child was 'Kishan'.

8

# Showing the Sun

After the naming, baby Kishan was taken to the door and briefly shown the sun. This is another Samskara: the sun is regarded as important since it is the power which is necessary to life, so this ritual of showing the child the sun for the first time is usually observed.

# Head Shaving

Another ceremony which is regarded as being of considerable importance, marking another stage in the development of the child is that at which the baby's hair is shaved off. This is usually done during the first year of its life.

Baby Kishan was three months old when the Patels invited their friends and relatives to attend the head shaving ceremony. They hired a hall for the occasion and set out tea and sweets for their guests to enjoy as they arrived.

One part of the hall had been specially set aside for the ceremony: carpets had

Ready for the head shaving

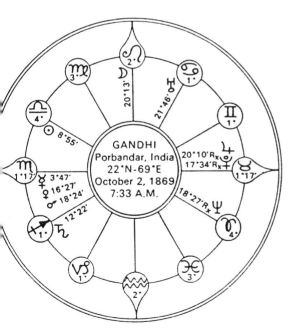

been laid down in this area and here two priests sat barefoot in front of a small shrine which included figures of some Hindu gods. The priests were chanting quietly and continuously in Sanskrit, an ancient Hindu language. Beside them on the floor, the special objects which would be used in the ceremony were laid out in readiness. There was a large silver tray, a pot of red dye, a bag of cereals, flowers, water and a pot of ghee (melted butter); there was also a brazier full of sticks ready for a fire to be lit.

When all the guests had arrived one of the priests took some red dye and drew a diagram on the tray; this is known as a **Mandala** and consists of a symbolic representation of the nine planets and other gods or sacred beings, e.g. Ganesha,

9

the elephant god, and Suraj Devata, the sun. While reciting lines from the Sanskrit text open in front of him, the priest directed the parents in the worship of the gods represented by the symbols. To each, in turn, the prepared substances were offered – water, camphor and flowers – by placing them on the tray.

The next part of the Puja (the name given to an act of worship at a shrine) was **Havan**, the offering of fire. The priests took some of the ghee and poured it on to the sticks in the brazier; the fire soon kindled and blazed up.

Fire is an important aspect of worship in Hinduism since it is thought to take the offerings to the gods; it also consumes and wipes out evil and gives the chance of a fresh start. Each parent took a spoon and placed more ghee on the fire. They also took a plate of cereal at intervals and made offerings of it in the hope of blessings for Kishan.

When this part of the worship was over, everyone joined in a Bhajan, a hymn of praise:

Putting ghee on the fire

'Peace be in the higher worlds
Peace be in the firmament
Peace be on earth.
May all be in peace and only peace
And may that peace come unto me.
Om, shanti, shanti, shanti, shanti.'
(Lord God, bring peace, peace, peace, peace.)

It was then time for the actual cutting of the hair; Kishan's grandfather as head of the household took his baby grandson in his arms and held him while the barber cut Kishan's hair.

As the hair was cut, Kishan's aunt carefully collected it in a plate. The hair would either be buried or placed in a stream together with the articles included in the first part of the ceremony. This ensures that the substances offered to the gods will not be treated lightly by coming into contact with any unworthy objects.

Some of the words recited during the hair shaving ceremony, when they were translated for us, gave us an insight into what it was all about:

'May God remove disease from this child.'
'I perform this ceremony to make you attain life, power, wealth and strength.'
'I cut your hair for your long life, fame and prosperity.'
'O barber, cleanse the head of this child!'

It was explained to us that Hindus believe that each of us has lived previous lives on earth; the **Atman** or 'soul' is regarded as undying; the physical body may die but the soul lives on to be born again, and this belief is called **Reincarnation**. (You will learn more about this when you come to consider views about death on page 105.)

Hindus also have a belief which they call **Karma**. At its simplest this may be described as a belief that every action brings a result. An individual may not have to face the results of all his actions

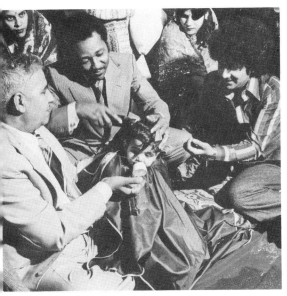
The head is shaved

good start in life and cleanse away, as far as possible, any bad influence from a previous existence.

*Task 1*
Briefly explain the following terms which occur in the account of Hindu birth ceremonies: Samskara, Aum, Mandala, Havan, Atman, Karma.

*Task 2*
Write a conversation between a Hindu girl or boy whose baby brother has recently had his hair shaved off at a ceremony like the one described in this chapter, and a non-Hindu friend. In your account not only describe the ceremony but try to answer questions about why such a ceremony is important.

in this life but he may reap the result of them in a future life when his soul is reborn. Head shaving of a child is related to those beliefs: it shows the parents' belief that this baby Kishan has lived previous lives on earth, but since he is now in their care they wish to give him a

*Task 3*
The Bhajan sung in Kishan's ceremony (page 10) seems to express some hopes about the kind of life Kishan will have: write a poem which expresses hopes you might have for the life of a recently born baby.

The hair collected for burning

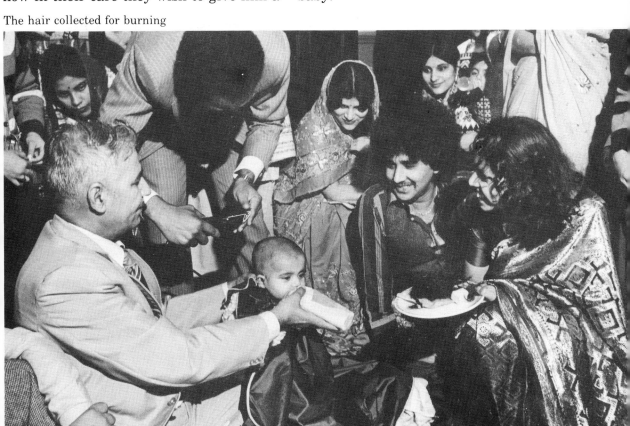

# 2

# Jewish

This Jewish family and their friends are celebrating a very happy occasion: eight days ago a son was born and the arrival of this, their first child, has made them very happy indeed. As the parents have talked together during these last few days, they have remembered the words of the scriptures given to their forefathers, 'Be fruitful and multiply', and they have given thanks to God that they now have a child. They have also remembered the tradition reflected in their scriptures that, when a son was born, a messenger was sent at once to bring the news to the father. The messenger would cry out, 'a man-child is born to you!' and there would be great rejoicing. Today is particularly important because, being the eighth day since the birth, the ceremony of **Brit Milah** is to take place. At this ceremony the baby boy is circumcised, i.e. a small piece of skin covering the tip of the baby's penis is cut away. This is a very simple operation for an infant, for which little or no anaesthetic is required. Even some non-Jews have this done for health reasons, but for Jews it is not done on health grounds but for very important religious reasons.

# Brit Milah

We asked the father about this ceremony and what it meant to his family and to the child:

*Our question:* This is clearly a very important day for you and your family, but it involves what some might consider to be a very strange ceremony indeed – the performing of this minor surgical operation on your baby son. Can you explain this for us?

*Answer:* This ceremony, known as Brit Milah, has been practised by our people for over 4,000 years and is of great religious significance to us. Brit and Milah are Hebrew words and mean literally, 'covenant of circumcision'. A covenant, as you know, is an agreement between two or more persons or groups to do, or indeed not to do, some specific action. We Jews believe that our scriptures tell us of three important covenants made between God and our people:

(1) God made a covenant with Noah after the flood, according to the story in the Book of Genesis. God said he would never again destroy the earth with a flood. In return, Noah must agree to live by God's law. The story says that the sign of this covenant was a rainbow in the sky.

(2) God made a covenant with Moses that, so long as Moses and his people kept the Ten Commandments which God gave to Moses, God would protect and guide his people. We Jews still regard this as important, and the signs of this covenant are the tablets of stone with the Ten Commandments which you can see portrayed in every Jewish synagogue; another sign of it is our observance of the Sabbath.

(3) The third covenant is the one which is important for our ceremony today: a covenant was made between God and our great forefather, Abraham. He believed that God promised him that he would be the father of a great nation and that God would forever be his God and the God of his descendants. As a sign that they were God's special people, Abraham and his descendants were to circumcise every male born to them.

*Our question:* So today's ceremony for your baby son is a very ancient one indeed?

*Answer:* It certainly is! We Jews have practised this since the days of Abraham. When we do this, we are bringing our sons into the covenant of Abraham and are obeying what we have been told to do in our scriptures. Sometimes it has been extremely dangerous for our people to be identified as Jews; for example in Nazi Germany under Adolf Hitler six million Jews were destroyed. However, even when the sign of circumcision puts our people's lives in danger we still observe this ceremony and will continue to do so in obedience to God.

*Our question:* Jews are not the only people to practise circumcision. There are those who would say that it originated as a fertility rite, that primitive people believed that if this was done it would ensure that the males would be able to father more children. Has this anything to do with your ideas about circumcision?

*Answer:* No! I recognise, of course, this kind of primitive origin of such a practice, but for us it is a sign of great religious significance. We are doing it because we are God's people.

*Our question:* Why do you carry out the circumcision on the eighth day after the birth of the child?

*Answer:* Quite simply because we believe it was in God's instructions about this sign of our covenant with him. Our scriptures, in Genesis chapter 17 verse

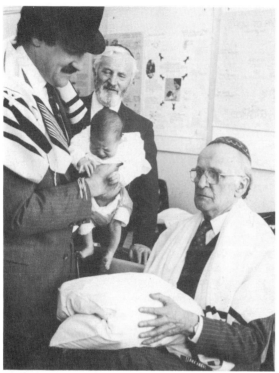

The baby placed on the Sandek's knee

12, say this should be done when a baby boy is eight days old. It is so important to us that even if the eighth day falls on the Sabbath it will still be carried out. Usually the only circumstance in which it will be delayed is if the child is unwell. In this case it would be done as soon as possible after the eighth day.

*Task 1*

(a) Circumcision is described as a sign of a covenant; briefly explain what a covenant is.

Other words which describe types of covenant are: treaty; contract; guarantee; what persons or groups would be involved in each of these contracts?

(b) Look up Genesis chapter 17 verses 1 to 14 in your Bible. This passage is presented as a conversation between Abraham and God; select the main parts of the conversation and express them in your own words.

(c) Circumcision will be performed on the eighth day after birth even if that day is the Sabbath. How does this indicate the importance of circumcision to Jews?

**Observing the Ceremony**

The ceremony can take place either at home or at a hospital. In this case it was in a room at the local hospital. The room had been prepared as you can see from the photograph on page 12; a table was set out with two candles and some wine; a chair was set aside and referred to as 'Elijah's chair'. The **Mohel** had arrived: he is the person who performs the operation; he need not be a doctor, but he will certainly be specially qualified. Usually, as in the case of a synagogue service, at least ten men are present and you can see that it was so on this occasion. You will notice that the mother has no part in this ceremony, but, as you can see in the photograph on page 16, she is present.

The father made a declaration that he was presenting his son for circumcision as commanded by the Almighty. He said that in order to follow the tradition he ought to be performing the operation, but as he was not qualified to do so he wanted the Mohel to do it for him.

The baby's grandfather was given the privilege of taking his new grandson and placing him for a moment in Elijah's chair. As he did so, he said, 'This is the throne of Elijah: may he be remembered for good!' Elijah was one of the early prophets and on an occasion such as this, Jews refer to him as 'the protector of children'. Many also refer to a story about Elijah, told in 1 Kings chapter 19, when the prophet was feeling very depressed and prayed to God, 'Lord God Almighty, I have always served you – you alone. But the people of Israel have broken their covenant with you. . .I am the only one left!' By placing the child on Elijah's chair, they are signifying –

'Look! Here are some Jews who are obeying the Covenant!'

Next, the father took his son and placed him on the knees of a close and well-respected friend of the family. In this ceremony he is known as the **Sandek**. Some Jews in fact use another word which means 'godfather'. It is a great honour to be asked to be Sandek and parents usually choose someone whom they consider will be a good example to their child as he grows up.

Before performing the circumcision, the Mohel prayed, 'Blessed art thou, O Lord our God, King of the Universe, who has sanctified us by thy commandments and hast commanded us concerning the circumcision.'

The Mohel then carefully performed the circumcision. When it was done, the father said, 'Blessed art thou, O Lord our God, King of the Universe, who hast sanctified us by thy commandments, and hast commanded us to make our sons enter into the covenant of Abraham our Father.'

The Rabbi, or minister of the synagogue, then offered some other prayers, in the course of which the baby was named. He said, 'Our God and God of our Fathers,

Performing circumcision

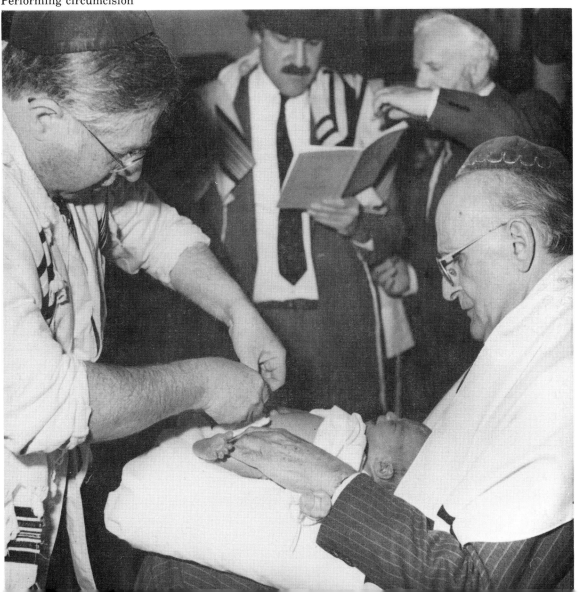

preserve this child to his father and to his mother, and let his name be called in Israel, Jacob son of Samuel.' On every religious occasion from now on, that name will be used in Hebrew for baby Jacob.

When the prayer was ended, the Rabbi took a cup of wine and gave some to the Sandek; a few drops of it were also given to baby Jacob and the mother was given a sip from the cup. Wine is used at most Jewish ceremonies and is simply a reminder that each is a happy occasion.

## The Birth of a Girl

If the baby had been a girl there would have been no Brit Milah. Instead, on the first Sabbath after the birth at the synagogue service, the father would have been 'called up' to the Bimah from where the Torah scroll is read to the congregation. While he is at the Bimah the Hebrew name for his daughter is announced to those present. (Being 'called up to the Torah' is a great honour, and one who is 'called up' stands on the right-hand side of the man who on that day will read from the Torah.)

*Task 2*

(a) Describe the role of each of the main participants in the ceremony of circumcision. What features make this far more than just a minor surgical operation?

(b) You will notice that the men in the photographs have their heads covered and the main participants in the ceremony are wearing a Tallith, i.e. a prayer shawl. Why do you think this is so, even though they are not at a synagogue service?

(c) As the father or mother of the child, explain why you thought it was important to have this ceremony for your child.

## The Redemption of the First-born

There is another Jewish birth ceremony which only applies in the following circumstances:

(1) The child born is the first to be born to the woman, who must not previously have had any miscarriage.

(2) The child is a boy.

This ceremony is known by the Hebrew name of **Pidyan Haben** and takes place on the thirty-first day after the boy is

The Sandek drinks the wine

born; it is often carried out in the family home.

The story behind this ceremony is that in early Biblical times all first-born males were said to belong to God and were dedicated to his service to act as priests, musicians or to serve in other ways in the Temple. Even the first-born of animals, if male, were sacrificed because they were regarded as sacred to God. Later, those belonging to the tribe of Levi were appointed to carry out Temple duties, and so the custom developed that parents of a first-born boy, instead of giving him to serve in the Temple, paid a sum of money to buy him back; the money was paid to a member of the tribe of Levi, until the Temple in Jerusalem was destroyed in the year 70 C.E.

The ceremony is still conducted and someone known as **Cohen**, i.e. someone who is descended from the priestly families who used to serve in the Temple, is present. In the ceremony, the father presents the baby to this man and at the same time places before him five silver coins known as shekels. (In 1974, the Bank of Israel began to produce special 'redemption' coins and it was five of these which were used on this occasion.)

Five shekels

The Cohen says to the father: 'Which would you rather: give me your first-born son, the first born of his mother, or redeem him for five shekels which you are bound to give according to the Law?'

The father replies, 'I desire rather to redeem my son and here you have the value of the redemption which I am bound to give according to the Law.'

After returning the child to the father and taking the money, certain prayers are offered, then, with the father and the Rabbi looking on, the Cohen places his hands in blessing on the child's head and says the following prayer of blessing:

'The Lord bless thee and keep thee: the Lord make his face to shine upon thee, and be gracious unto thee: the Lord turn his face unto thee, and give thee peace.

The Lord is thy guardian: the Lord is thy shade upon thy right hand. For length of days, and years of life and peace shall they add to thee. The Lord shall guard thee from evil; he shall guard thy soul. Amen.'

It must be understood, of course, that there is no question of the Cohen taking away the child if the parents do not pay!

Nowadays, the Cohen usually donates the value of the silver coins to some Jewish charity.

*Task 3*
According to Exodus chapter 13 verses 11 to 16, another reason for the Redemption of the First-born has to do with the Israelites' escape from Egypt under the leadership of Moses.

(a) Look up these verses and also Exodus chapter 12 verses 1 to 13 and write a brief account of the event to which they refer. At which annual festival is this event especially remembered?

(b) What do you think this birth ceremony tells us about the attitude which Jews have towards God?

# 3

# Christian

All Christian Churches (i.e. Christian groups or 'denominations') have a ceremony in which the importance of the birth of a baby is recognised. In the majority, this ceremony involves the symbolic act of baptism which will be explored in the next few pages. Another important aspect of the ceremony is that the baby is named; some people call it 'christening', i.e. the occasion when the baby is given publicly its 'Christian' names.

The baby is baptised

# Baptism

Mr and Mrs Cook have recently had twin boys; they have chosen the names Richard and Andrew, and they would like their children to be baptised into the Christian faith and to grow up in this faith.

Although it is the baby who is baptised, clearly the decision to have the ceremony is one which is made by the parents. For this reason the Reverend George Frost, the Vicar at the Cooks' place of worship, considers it important for parents to be aware of the responsibility they are taking when they have their children baptised. He therefore invites them to his home to discuss the service and what is involved. We went along with Mr and Mrs Cook and several other parents to find out about the ceremony. In the course of the evening we were able to obtain answers to several of our questions which we put to Revd Frost.

*Our question:* What, in your opinion, is the purpose of infant baptism?

*Answer:* It is an opportunity for parents to dedicate their baby to God, to thank God and to make a promise to bring up the child as a practising Christian. Baptism is really a first step into the Church.

*Our question:* What do you consider is the most important thing you have said to parents in this preparation class?

*Answer:* I think it is very important that they are fully aware of what they are doing when they bring their children for baptism, but perhaps the most important idea I have explored with them is that their example, as parents, will be the most significant factor in the child's growth as a Christian.

*Our question:* You have mentioned in your talk to these parents that they require 'godparents' for their children when they bring them for baptism: can you explain the purpose of such godparents?

*Answer:* Before coming to the ceremony, parents choose friends or relatives who will be godparents for the child. If the baby is a boy it is usual to choose two godfathers and one godmother; if a girl it is usual to have two godmothers and one godfather. Godparents are usually friends of the family who are willing to be especially friendly to the child and to be a good example and so help with its Christian upbringing. They make certain baptismal promises on behalf of the child and they are expected to pray regularly for the child. It is hoped they will encourage the child to grow in the faith so that a time will come when he or she will ask for a ceremony of Confirmation, i.e. a ceremony in which the child confirms his or her own decision to follow Christ.

*Our question:* What is the most important part of the ceremony of baptism?

*Answer:* The essential part of a Holy Baptism is the pouring of water on the head of the child with the words, 'I baptise you in the name of the Father and of the Son and of the Holy Spirit.' This is something which has been practised by the Christian Church, in one way or another, since the days of the early Church and is seen as an act symbolising introduction into the Church.

## The Baptismal Service

The baptism of Richard and Andrew Cook took place on a Sunday afternoon. A special service had been arranged and Mr and Mrs Cook joined seven other sets of parents with their families and friends in the church. Everyone was gathered near the **font**.

A font is a container for water which is used in the baptism. In many old churches the font is at the rear of the church by the entrance to remind Christians as they enter that baptism is the first step in the faith. The font in the photograph used to be in such a position by the door but it has been moved to a position where it can more easily be seen by all who are present at a baptism.

As the service proceeded, our minds went back to what we had heard at the preparation class about the important role of parents and godparents at a baptism. They were required to make three public declarations about their faith before the babies were baptised.

Standing by the font, the Revd Frost said, 'The children whom you have brought for baptism chiefly depend on you for the help and encouragement they need. Are you willing to give it to them by your prayers, by your example and by your teaching?'

The parents replied together, 'Yes, I am willing.'

Prayers were offered and then came the second declaration: the Vicar addressed the parents and godparents: 'I ask these questions which you must answer for yourselves and for these children.'

*Question:* Do you turn to Christ?
*Response:* I turn to Christ.
*Question:* Do you repent of your sins?
*Response:* I repent of my sins.
*Question:* Do you renounce evil?
*Response:* I renounce evil.

Finally the parents and godparents were required to answer three questions about their belief:

'Do you believe and trust in God, the Father, who made the world?
Do you believe and trust in his Son, Jesus Christ, who redeemed mankind?
Do you believe and trust in his Holy Spirit, who gives life to the people of God?'

To each question they replied, 'I believe and trust in him.'

Each child was baptised individually; as the name was called out by the Vicar,

each father carried his child to the font and placed the baby in the Vicar's arms, while the mothers and godparents stood nearby.

The Vicar poured a little water over the child's forehead as he named the child and said, 'I baptise you in the name of the Father and the Son and the Holy Spirit. I sign you with the Cross, the sign of Christ. Do not be ashamed to confess the faith of Christ crucified.' As he said these last words, he made the shape of a cross in water on the baby's forehead. At this point in each baptism, the congregation called out:

'Fight valiantly under the banner of Christ against sin, the world and the devil and continue his faithful soldier and servant to the end of your life.'

In this particular church it is the custom to give the mother a candle when a child is baptised. A large candle was burning by the font and the Revd Frost took a small candle and lit it from the large one. As he handed it to the mother he said, 'Receive this light: this is to show you that you have passed from darkness to light.'

The congregation said, 'Shine like a light in the world.'

When all the babies had been baptised, they were welcomed into the Church by the members of the congregation.

To mark this special occasion which was a first step in Christianity for Richard and Andrew, the Cooks were given a certificate of baptism.

*Task 1*
As a godparent, describe your duties in the service of baptism and the promises you make. How do you think you can fulfil these duties as the child grows up?

*Task 2*
Using the photograph as a guide, make your own drawing of a baptismal font. Explain clearly what is said and done at

After the baptism

the font during the baptismal service.

*Task 3*
What do you consider to be the symbolism of a candle being given to the mother after the baptism?

# An Infant Dedication

It is not every Christian group which has a ceremony of baptism for babies. Mr and Mrs Parkes are Christians but in their Church it is the custom to bring a recently born baby for what is called a service of Infant Dedication. Although the child is not baptised, nevertheless such Christians believe it is important to have a ceremony to mark the birth of each child at which it is also named.

We talked to the Minister of Mr and Mrs Parkes' church and asked him questions about this service of dedication.
*Our question:* Most Christian Churches baptise a baby; why is it that you don't do this?
*Answer:* We believe that baptism has more meaning when the person being baptised is old enough to ask for it and to understand what it is all about. We think that this is what happened in the early Church which we read about in the Bible.
*Our question:* Is your service of dedication, then, just an attempt to satisfy parents that they are not losing out, since you will not baptise their babies?
*Answer:* Not at all! We, in common with other Christians and indeed, in common with most people, regard the birth of a child as a tremendously important event in the lives of the parents and, of course, for the child itself! We believe therefore that it is very important for parents to be able to bring their baby to a ceremony in church in which they can thank God for the gift of a child and ask for the prayers of the Church to enable them to fulfil their responsibilities as parents. It is also important to have such an occasion when, publicly in the church service, the child is given its 'Christian' name – the name chosen for it by the parents.

## The Service of Dedication

We were present at the service when Mr and Mrs Parkes brought their baby daughter to church. The dedication took place at the end of the morning worship.

The parents came and stood facing the Minister, by the Communion-table at the front of the church; Mrs Parkes was carrying their baby, who was lying very quietly in her arms. We noticed that, whereas in the baptism described earlier there were godparents standing with the parents, on this occasion there were only the parents; we remembered that the Minister had told us that this ceremony concerns the parents, the baby and the Church as a whole.

The dedication began with the Minister saying, 'We welcome in the name of the Lord, Mr and Mrs Parkes and their baby daughter. We are gathered together at their request to present this child before God, to give thanks with them for the gift of this new life, to unite our prayers

Infant dedication

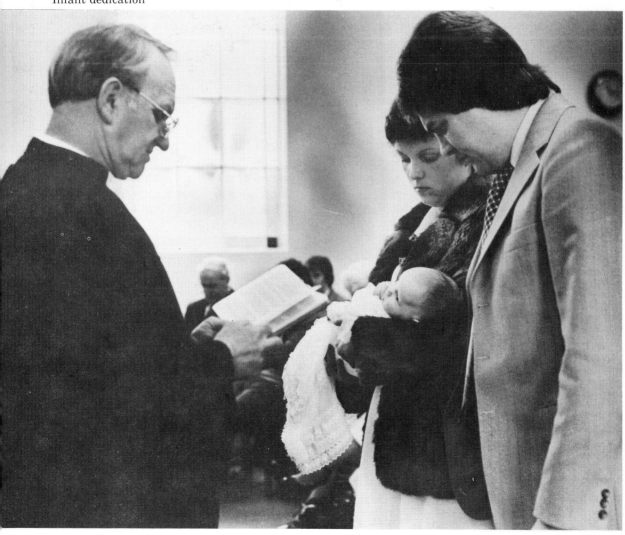

'The Lord bless you and keep you'

with theirs that God will guide and strengthen them in the responsibilities of parenthood and to ask God's blessing on their child.'

The Minister read some verses from the Bible about children and parents and then he addressed questions to the parents:

'In the name of the Church, I ask you: do you acknowledge with gratitude the goodness of God in the gift of this child, and do you accept the responsibility which comes with the gift to give your child a Christian upbringing?'

The parents responded by saying, 'We do.'

They were then asked, 'Will you endeavour by God's help, so to order your home life that your child will be surrounded by Christian example and influence?'

The parents responded, 'We will.'

The Minister then addressed the congregation and said that if they accepted the responsibility to welcome and help, in whatever way possible, these parents and their child, they should signify this by standing.

With everyone standing, he took the baby in his arms and said:

'Lynsey Jane, the Lord bless you and keep you: the Lord make his face to shine upon you and be gracious to you: the Lord lift up his countenance upon you and give you peace. Amen.'

He handed the baby back to the father and then led everyone in a prayer for the parents and their baby.

Mr and Mrs Parkes were given a certificate to mark this important occasion in the life of their baby daughter.

*Task 4*

(a) List the differences between the service of baptism for a baby, and that of dedication. What similarities are there?

(b) What advantages and what disadvantages do you see in each ceremony (i) for the parents, and (ii) for the baby?

Dedication certificate

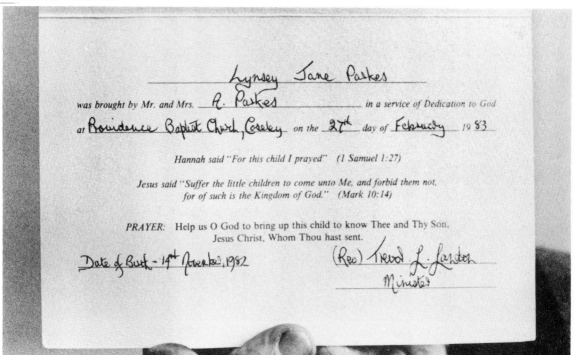

Lynsey Jane Parkes

was brought by Mr. and Mrs. R. Parkes _____ in a service of Dedication to God

at Providence Baptist Church, Coseley on the 27th day of February 19 83

Hannah said "For this child I prayed"  (1 Samuel 1:27)

Jesus said "Suffer the little children to come unto Me, and forbid them not, for of such is the Kingdom of God."  (Mark 10:14)

PRAYER: Help us O God to bring up this child to know Thee and Thy Son, Jesus Christ, Whom Thou hast sent.

Date of Birth - 14th November, 1982

(Rev) Trevor L. Laxton

Minister

# 4
# Muslim

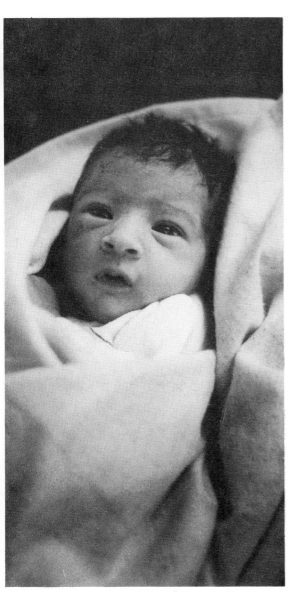

Mr and Mrs Khan were very happy indeed for a son had been born to them. Muslims believe that children are a gift from Allah (God) and they consider themselves honoured to be entrusted with the responsibility of a new life. These parents were a little anxious at first for their baby son was born prematurely and had to be cared for in hospital for a time. News of the birth was sent to the Imam, the leader of the local Muslim community, and he came to conduct a very simple ceremony which is important to Muslims whenever a child has been born. This ceremony can be performed by any Muslim man but, in this case, it was carried out by the Imam from the local mosque. Because such care was being taken since the baby was rather weak, the Imam and Mr Khan had to put on white hospital gowns.

## The First Ceremony

We watched carefully to see what would happen in this simple ceremony. After greeting Mr and Mrs Khan and congratulating them on the birth of their son, the Imam bent down over the baby and whispered words into his right ear. He was speaking in Arabic, the religious language of Islam, and the words were:

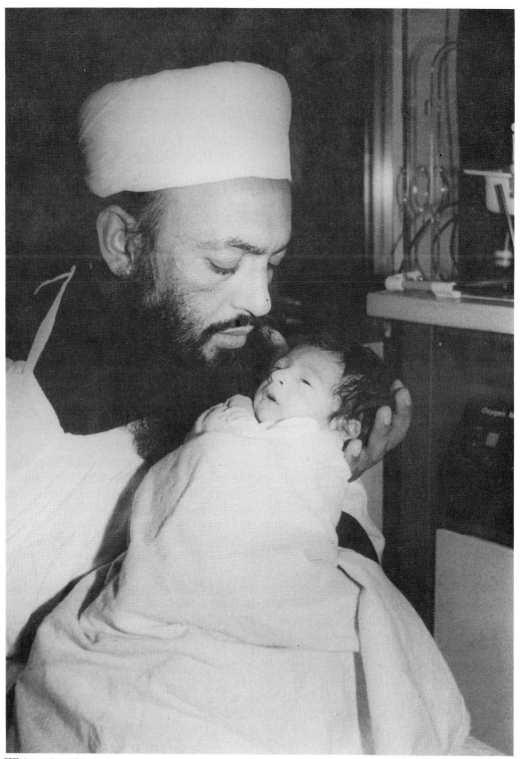

Whispering the Adhan

Allahu Akbar
Allahu Akbar
Allahu Akbar
Allahu Akbar
Ash-hadu an la ilaha illallah
Ash-hadu an la ilaha illallah
Ash-hadu anna Muhammadu rasulullah
Ash-hadu anna Muhammadu rasulullah
Hayye alas salah
Hayye alas salah
Hayye alal falah
Hayye alal falah
Allahu Akbar
Allahu Akbar
La ilaha illallah

These are the words which sound out from the mosque five times every day, calling the worshippers to prayer. The words are known as the **Adhan** and mean:

God is the greatest
God is the greatest
God is the greatest
God is the greatest
I bear witness that there is no God but Allah
I bear witness that there is no God but Allah
I bear witness that Muhammad is the messenger of Allah
I bear witness that Muhammad is the messenger of Allah
Come to prayer
Come to prayer
Come to security
Come to security
God is the greatest
God is the greatest
There is no God but Allah

The Imam then held the child so that he could whisper into its left ear similar words known as the **Iqamat**.

When we asked about the ceremony, we were told that, of course, the child could not understand the words but it is their way of acknowledging that Allah has given them the gift of a child and they are symbolising their desire to introduce the child, at the earliest possible moment, to the faith which means so much to them. We were also told that some Muslims believe that once this has been done, the child will be protected by Allah from any harm.

We asked Mr Khan if there was any ceremony in which the baby would be named. 'Oh yes!' he replied, 'that usually takes place on the seventh day after the birth. You are welcome to come and see that also.'

# The Naming Ceremony – Aqiqah

We returned to the home of the Khan family when the baby was well enough to go home. Other friends and relatives had gathered and everyone seemed very happy and anxious to see the new baby.

In the first part of the ceremony the baby's hair has to be shaved off to symbolise the baby being purified; we were also told that it makes the hair grow thicker! The Imam showed Mr Khan how to do this, then Mrs Khan held the baby while her husband did the shaving. The hair was weighed: it did not weigh very much! This is done because, traditionally, the family, if they can afford it, give an equivalent amount in gold or silver, or just a sum of money, to a charity which helps people in need. Usually the amount given is considerably more than the weight of the hair!

In the next part of the ceremony the Imam took the child in his arms while Mr Khan looked proudly at his son: the Imam spoke the name of the child, 'Rashid' which means 'guide' and is one of the ninety-nine names which Muslims give to Allah. Also at this time, the Imam again whispered the words of the Adhan, the call to prayer, in the ear of the child.

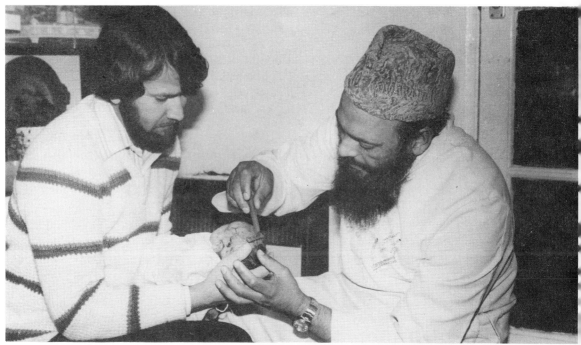

The Imam begins the head shaving

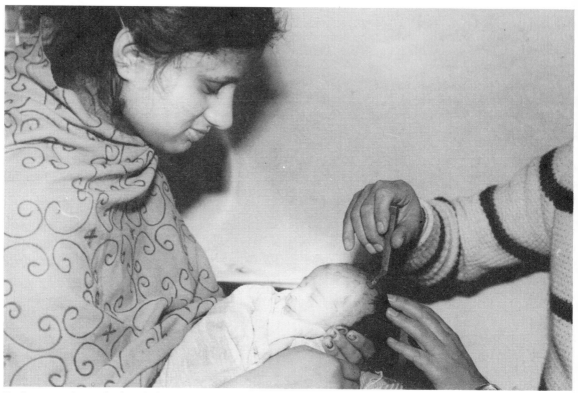

Father completes the head shaving

Naming the child

## Circumcision

Muslims also observe a custom which they have in common with Jews: baby boys are circumcised. You can read about this in the section on Judaism on page 12. Muslims usually carry out this simple operation as part of the Aqiqah ceremony and this was quickly done for Rashid by their family doctor who is also a Muslim.

After all this had been done, a meal was provided for all the guests and, in conversation, we discovered some other aspects of what we had witnessed.

## Choosing the Name

We were told that customs vary as far as the choice of name is concerned: sometimes the decision is left to the head of the family, who quite often will be the baby's grandfather; sometimes it is a privilege given to the father's sister; sometimes it is quite simply chosen by the father and mother themselves.

Regardless of who makes the choice, the name is usually chosen from a list of great Muslims of the past, or from names of members of the Prophet Muhammad's own family. It may be one of the prophets who lived before Muhammad, who are named in the Qur'an, or it may be, as in the case of baby Rashid, chosen from one of the ninety-nine personal names which Muslims have for Allah, e.g. instead of being given a name which means 'guide' he might have been given a name meaning, 'the Merciful One', 'the King', or 'the Holy One'; the name would of course have been in Arabic. (For a full list of the ninety-nine names for Allah, see our book *Believers*, page 33.)

Girls may also be named in a similar way; the name may be chosen from a list of well-known Muslim women, e.g. Fatima, Nabila, Rahila, Aisha.

# Sacrifice

Years ago, primitive people used to sacrifice animals to God to show their gratitude for some special occasion. On the birth of a Muslim child it was the custom to sacrifice two sheep if the child was male and one if it was female. Mr Khan observed this ancient custom by asking a Muslim butcher to slaughter two sheep and then arranged for the meat to be given to poor families. Some Muslims say that this sacrifice is to save the child from any future disaster: others regard it as a way of saying 'thank you' for the gift of a child.

# Four Years Old – Bismillah

We were told of another ceremony which would take place when Rashid reached the age of four. As soon as he is old enough, he will be taught the letters of the Arabic alphabet so that he can recite simple sentences from the Qur'an. The hope is that on his fourth birthday he will be able to recite the sentence which begins with the Arabic word 'Bismillah':

'Bismillahi ar Rahman ar Rahim'
(In the Name of Allah, the Compassionate, the Merciful)

So, when the time comes, at the family party for Rashid's fourth birthday, he will probably recite this to his friends and members of the family and they will make a fuss of him, giving him gifts and letting him see how proud they are of him. From this time on he will be taught more and more about what it means to be a Muslim so that, at an early age, the faith by which his parents live will become just as important to him.

*Task 1*
Give brief answers to the following questions:
   (a) How is a Muslim child's name chosen?
   (b) Why is the hair shaved?
   (c) How old is the child when it is named?
   (d) What aspects of the naming ceremony show that giving to charity is an important feature of Islam?
   (e) What happens at a Muslim child's fourth birthday?

*Task 2*
Imagine that you know nothing about Muslim beliefs, but you have witnessed the birth ceremonies described in this section. What would you have learned from them about important beliefs held by Muslims?

*Task 3*
When Muslims pray they offer certain set prayers but also their own personal prayers. Bearing in mind what you have learned about important Muslim beliefs, write a prayer which a Muslim father or mother might pray around the time of the child's birth ceremonies.

*Task 4*
Write out the words of the Muslim call to prayer. What do you think is the value of these words being used in the Muslim birth ceremony despite the fact that the child cannot understand?

# 5
# Sikh

Mr and Mrs Gill, along with other members of their family, have come to the gurdwara (i.e. the temple where Sikhs in our community meet for worship) for a very happy occasion. Recently, Mrs Gill has given birth to a son and they have come for a ceremony at which he will be named.

Preparing the Amrit

# The Naming Ceremony

Most parents usually spend some time discussing what name to give to their new-born baby; a name, after all, is very important since it is something which marks one out as a person for the rest of life. Sikh parents consider the choice of a name to be so important that they allow their holy book, known as the Guru Granth Sahib, to guide them in their choice.

The special ceremony for the baby takes place at the end of the normal service of worship. Parents come and present their baby before the sacred book. Quite often a hymn from the sacred book is read; on this occasion it is the one composed by one of the early Gurus of the Sikh faith, Guru Arjan, at the time of the birth of his son, Hargobind:

'The true God has sent the child,
The long-lived child has been born by destiny.
When he came and acquired an abode in the womb
His mother's heart became very glad.'

A mixture called **Amrit** has been prepared by dissolving sugar crystals in water. The Granthi (the man who sits behind the sacred book and who reads from it in worship) stirs the mixture with a **Khanda** – a short, two-edged sword. As he stirs, the Granthi recites the first five verses of the Japji, the most important prayer from the Guru Granth Sahib, which was composed by Guru Nanak, the founder of the Sikh religion.

When he has completed this prayer the Granthi puts the tip of a little sword known as a **Kirpan** into the Amrit and lightly touches the baby's tongue and the top of the baby's head with the Amrit; the remainder of the mixture is given to the mother to drink.

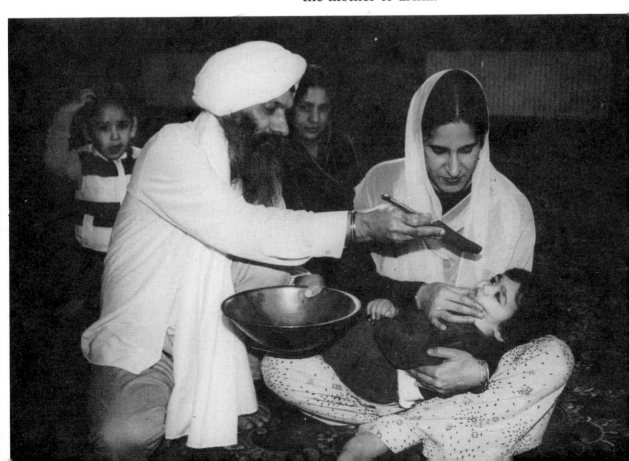

The sacred book

The other very important part of the ceremony is when the Granthi opens the sacred book at random and reads the first word on the left-hand page. It is then up to the parents to choose a name beginning with the same letter as that word. At this ceremony, once the parents knew the letter with which the name should begin, they spoke to the Granthi who then announced to the congregation that Mr and Mrs Gill had chosen the name Amarjit and he added another name, Singh, which is always a part of a Sikh boy's name; if the baby had been a girl, he would have added the name Kaur (see p.35). If the parents had not been able to think of a suitable name at the time, they could have gone away to think about it and returned the following week for the name to be announced to the congregation.

After the Granthi announced the name, he said, 'Jo bole so nihal' which means, 'the One who speaks is a blessed One'. The congregation replied to this by saying, 'Sat sri akal', which means, 'God is truth'.

Part of the prayer known as the Anand Sahib is then read and this is followed by the Ardas which is always the final prayer in a Sikh service. On this occasion the prayer ends with the words:

'I present this child and with thy grace, I administer to him the Amrit.
May he be a true Sikh.
May he devote himself to the service of his fellowmen and motherland.
May he be inspired with devotion!'

The ceremony then ends with everyone receiving Karah Parshad, a sweet food, a portion of which is always given to everyone present in a Sikh service. This is a symbol that all are equal.

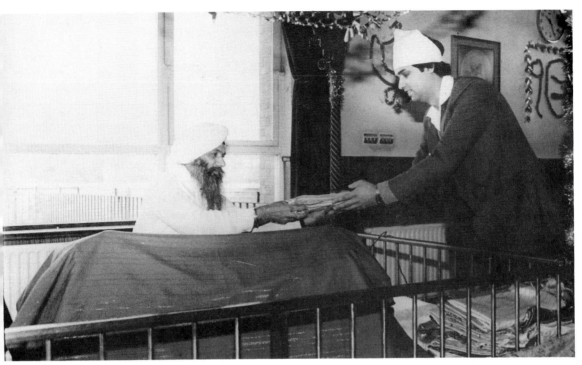

Presenting a Romalla

## Singh and Kaur

In addition to their other names, Sikh children are given another title: the name Singh is added for boys and Kaur for girls. Singh means 'lion' and Kaur means 'princess'. This practice has been carried out since the 17th century and was started by Guru Gobind Singh, who was the tenth and last Guru. He declared that after his death the sacred book, the Guru Granth Sahib, would be their teacher.

Guru Gobind Singh formed a brotherhood of Sikhs which was known as the **Khalsa**. He wanted all its members to be loyal to each other and completely united; they must put aside their differences and act as a family, no longer being divided by caste. The caste, or social group into which they had been born, decided their status and whether others would look up to them or look down on them. Guru Gobind Singh thought that by giving them a common name he would help rid the Sikhs of such distinctions and emphasise their equality. He chose the name Singh because he wanted them to be brave.

## Bringing Gifts

It is part of Sikh teaching that a child is a gift from God and should be welcomed as such. It is the custom for parents, when they come to the naming ceremony, to bring gifts to the gurdwara. Mr and Mrs Gill brought flour, sugar and butter which was used to prepare the Karah Parshad. Mrs Gill also brought a beautiful embroidered cloth which is known as a **Romalla**; her husband presented this and it will be used as a covering for the Guru Granth Sahib, which is so important in every Sikh act of worship. Gifts like these are ways in which Sikhs can express thanksgiving for the birth of their child. The Granthi accepted the Romalla and carefully spread it over the holy book.

## A First Step in the Faith

The naming ceremony for Amarjit Singh Gill is merely his first step in the Sikh faith. Guidance about his name has been given by the sacred book; he has been given a first taste of the Amrit; he has been given the added name of Singh to show he is equal with all the others. As he grows up, Amarjit will learn more and more of what it means to live according to the Sikh faith and, if he wishes to commit himself fully to it, a time will come when he will return for another important ceremony.

*Task 1*

What is the importance of the following at a Sikh naming ceremony?

(a) Guru Granth Sahib

(b) Amrit

(c) Khanda

(d) Karah Parshad

(e) Japji

*Task 2*

What do you think the practice of using the holy book as a guide to the choice of a name tells us about how Sikhs regard the book?

*Task 3*

Describe in your own words how Mr and Mrs Gill chose their child's name and compare it with the way your name was chosen.

*or*

Conduct an interview with Mr and Mrs Gill; write the answers you imagine they would give to the following questions:

(a) What is Amrit and how is it prepared?

(b) How was your baby's name chosen?

(c) Why was he also given the name Singh?

(d) What gifts did you bring to the gurdwara?

(e) What were the prayers which were said?

(f) What will you do to teach your child the Sikh faith?

(g) Why did you consult the holy book about the name?

# Additional Tasks on Birth Ceremonies

1 What features are common to the majority of the birth ceremonies you have studied? Why do you think they have so much in common, although they are ceremonies in different faiths?

2 (a) Why is the choice of a name so important? Find out how your parents chose your name and what that name means.

(b) Do you think it is a good idea to be named after another member of the family? Give reasons for your answer.

3 (a) Parents have to make many decisions for their children when they are young; do you consider that they should commit a child to a particular faith at that stage?

(b) Which of the birth ceremonies you have studied is likely to have the most effect on the child's future commitment to the faith of his parents? Give reasons for your answer.

4 What are the main responsibilities of parents towards their children? How are some of these responsibilities shown in the ceremonies you have studied?

5 Adherents of the faiths studied clearly considered their children to be 'gifts from God', i.e. each child was seen as a precious life for which they were now responsible.

(a) How does a parent's attitude towards a child affect its character?

(b) Which other people will influence the child as it grows?

# Part II
# Ceremonies of Commitment

# 5

# Hindu

When a Hindu boy reaches the age of eight he may be considered ready to take on the responsibilities of his religion, though if he is not thought to be ready this might be delayed till he is eleven. To mark this important stage in his life a ceremony may be held which is known as 'the investiture of the sacred thread' and he would begin to receive education about his religion from a guru, i.e. a religious teacher. He would be expected to show his commitment to his faith by leading a disciplined life and by studying the Hindu holy books.

Ancient Hindu holy books called 'The Laws of Manu', written approximately 200 BC, describe the rules which a boy would be expected to observe during this period of study:

'Let him have nothing to do with meat, perfumes, garlands, anger, jealousy, singing, dancing or playing musical instruments.

He may not gamble, lie, quarrel, hurt any living creature or associate with women.

The promise that he will study the holy books under a teacher must be kept until he has perfectly learned them.'

In the days when these rules were written a boy was expected to leave home to receive this education from his guru. Over the years, however, customs have changed to suit the conditions in which people live, but the ceremony did continue to be widely practised among Hindu families in the top three castes until recent times.

Ancient Hindus believed that society could be divided into four classes – priests, rulers, traders and peasants. An individual's position in life was decided by the fact of his birth into one of these groups: these groups came to be known as 'castes'. The sacred thread ceremony was practised among the priests, rulers and traders, but especially among the priests.

## The Sacred Thread Ceremony

We visited Mr Bhari, a Hindu living in our community, to discover more about this ceremony. He told us that it was known as **Upanayana** and in it the boy would be given a thread consisting of two separate links, each with three main cotton threads and each thread having three strands. Mr Bhari said that he wore this over his left shoulder and it was tied below waist level on the right-

hand side. In the photographs, a young Hindu boy is holding the thread to show the two links and then wearing it in the position Mr Bhari described (page 40).

We asked Mr Bhari about the significance of the threads and he explained that for him each strand stood for one of the three main gods of Hinduism: Brahma, the Creator; Vishnu, the God of Love and the Preserver of Life; and Shiva, the Destroyer. He also reminded us that many Hindus regard these three as different ways in which the One God has shown himself. Wearing the thread helped Mr Bhari to remember that he is always surrounded by God's presence: it was also a reminder of the truth and the value of the faith into which he had been initiated. Some other Hindus say that the strands are a reminder that they must control body, mind and speech.

We asked Mr Bhari to describe the ceremony for us and he told us of the time, many years before, when he had

gone through this ceremony:

'My initiation ceremony took place when I was eleven years old; when my family and I were living in India. My father consulted the astrologer who had cast my horoscope when I was born and he gave advice about the best time and place for the ceremony to take place. Invitations were sent out to family and friends; ten Brahmins, or priests, who lived in our neighbourhood were welcomed to our home. According to the custom, my father gave them food and money.

'Before the ceremony, my head was shaved since this was believed to be an aid to learning and was thought to be a sign of discipline. I bathed and put on new clothes so that I was perfectly clean in preparation for this special act of worship.

'In the courtyard of our home, a special canopy with four pillars had been erected for the occasion. I sat in my place under the canopy with the priests and I listened

38

to their chanting in Sanskrit the verses of our ancient scriptures.

'The person who conducts such a ceremony is known as the **archarya** and he becomes the boy's teacher. My archarya instructed me to say, "I will observe the discipline of celibacy": this meant that I was not to associate with girls during my period of study. When my studies were complete, I would of course be free to marry; indeed, it would be hoped that I would then marry.

'The thread was placed over my left shoulder and as it was tied, the archarya said, "This sacred thread is pure and will lead you to knowledge of God." The priests lit the sacrificial fire and I offered ghee, i.e. melted butter, to the fire and made my vows, saying, "I declare before you that I will observe all the vows and disciplines. May I prosper with that vow and attain the highest truth." Many other **mantras** or chants were said by my archarya but I remember best the final promises we made to each other. My archarya said, "I take your mind and heart into my control; grasp my words with affection and may God unite you with me in thought and action according to your vows from this day onwards."

'I replied, "I hold your mind and heart in me for the advancement of my study, learning and good actions. May God keep you always engaged in the task of my well-being."

'Indeed, the day I received my sacred thread was one of the most memorable days of my childhood. I still remember the good wishes of the guests as they departed: they said to me, "Grow in strength and vigour, live a hundred autumns."

'Now a period of study began; in fact it began that same day with a ceremony we call **Vedarambha**, the beginning of the study of the Vedas; these are the four oldest Hindu holy books. In this ceremony there was the recitation of the **Gayatri**

**Mantra** which is part of the Rig Veda (a book which has 1,017 hymns and was written about 1000 BC). "Let us meditate on the most excellent light of the Creator; may he guide our thoughts." This mantra is one which I most regularly repeat in worship.'

What Mr Bhari told us led us to ask more questions about the sacred thread ceremony:

*Our question:* Did the ceremony change your life in any way?

*Answer:* Yes, it most certainly did! I had to study hard to learn Sanskrit, the ancient language in which the Vedas are written, and to understand the ritual worship laid down in the holy books. I was now considered to be a man and could take a greater part in our acts of worship: I was now thought to be **Dvija** or 'twice-born': my second birth was a spiritual one given to me by my teacher for now I could begin to understand and grow in the faith.

*Our question:* Did all Hindu boys in your area receive the sacred thread?

*Answer:* No! Only those who belonged to the top three castes went through such a ceremony and wore the thread.

*Our question:* Is the thread ever removed?

*Answer:* It is only removed when it is renewed. Obviously continual use makes it wear thin and so it is changed each year in the month of August. In India, people gather by a lake or river in which they bathe three or four times and recite mantras before the priest gives them the new threads. It is a custom also that at this time they pray for their forefathers.

*Our question:* Is the thread always worn in the position you described to us, i.e. over the left shoulder and tied on the right side of the body?

*Answer:* The position of the thread may be altered for different ceremonies; for example, when praying for departed ancestors it is held at shoulder height.

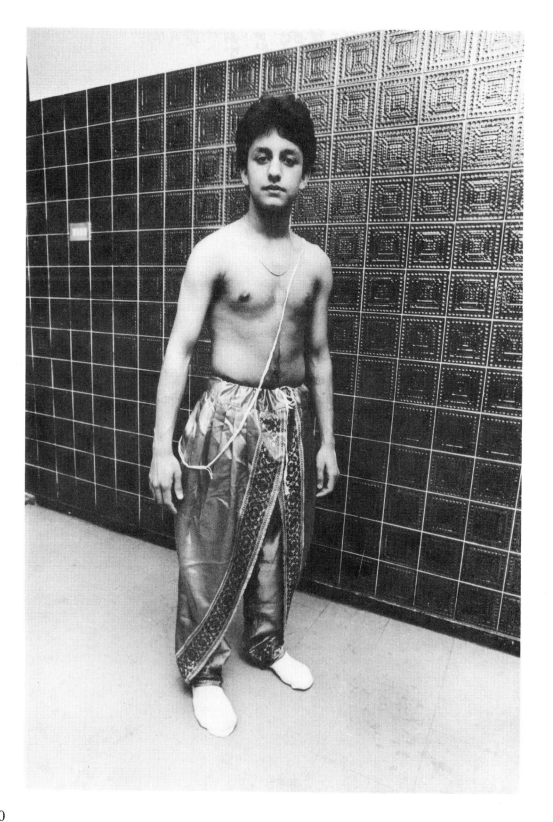

Our question: We were surprised to learn that many of the young Hindu boys in our community have not received the sacred thread. Can you explain why this is so?

Answer: In Hinduism, we believe that the world is in constant change and so some customs must be altered. Today, young people attend school and are seldom sent to learn from a spiritual teacher. Nevertheless, it is still the custom for many young men to receive the thread before they are married and this still shows their commitment to the Hindu faith and way of life.

# Living as a Hindu

Hinduism is often described as 'a way of life'; in other words, it is practically impossible to separate belief from behaviour. The true proof, therefore, of commitment to the faith is shown in everyday life, service to others, and worship in the home.

A visit to the home of the Bhari family could well show the way of life followed by the Hindu. On entering, it immediately becomes clear that it is impossible to separate religious practice from everyday life. Mr Bhari's son, Shiv, has a talent for design and he has decorated the home throughout with statues and pictures of the gods. The front room is a place of worship for the family who rise early each morning, bathe, and before eating breakfast, pray at the shrine. Mrs Bhari places offerings of food before the gods at the shrine and, after evening prayers, she gives each member of the family a portion of the food which is now regarded as **prashad**, or food which has been received by the gods.

The younger members of the family are taught how to pray and Mr Bhari tells them stories of the gods. The young, especially, learn from festivals which are celebrated and Mr Bhari involves them in dramatic presentations of stories from the holy books, which they act out for the Hindu community. The children learn that correct behaviour is important: Mr Bhari says, 'You have hands to use to do good; eyes which must see good things only; a mouth to speak wisely words of love; ears to hear the truth and legs to walk in the way of devotion.'

The whole family believes that service to others is of the greatest importance and they regularly help others in the area because they think that this is the Hindu way of life in practice.

*Task 1*
(a) What is the purpose of the wearing of a sacred thread by a Hindu?
(b) Describe the thread and explain what its three strands may represent.
(c) In what position is the thread worn?
(d) Why should the position be altered?
(e) When is the thread changed?

*Task 2*
Read the passage from The Laws of Manu on page 37 and write a description of the behaviour required from a boy who has received the thread.

*Task 3*
Imagine Mr Bhari kept a diary at the time of his sacred thread ceremony; write what you think his entry might have been at the end of the day when he received the thread.

*Task 4*
Guru Nanak, the founder of the Sikh faith, did not wear a sacred thread; instead, he said, 'I would wear a thread which has cotton of kindness, yarn of contentment, bonds of restraint and intertwining of truth.' What do you think of the Guru's attitude to the thread? Do you think Hindus would agree with the idea behind his words?

# 7
# Jewish

According to the Mishnah (important ancient Jewish writings which are not, however, part of their scriptures), a Jewish boy is thought to reach manhood when he is 13 years and one day; a girl is thought to reach womanhood when she is 12 years and one day. At that age, they are thought to be ready to accept the responsibilities of their religion.

As far as boys are concerned, it has been the custom for a long time to mark this important milestone in their lives by a ceremony known as **Bar Mitzvah**. Bar Mitzvah means 'a son of the commandment'. More recently, in some Jewish communities, the tradition has developed of having a similar type of ceremony for girls when they reach the age of twelve: this is known as **Bat Mitzvah** i.e. 'a daughter of the commandment'.

Rehearsal for Bar Mitzvah

Young people involved in these ceremonies are showing that they want to be committed to the Jewish faith and way of life. The Mishnah also says that at thirteen, a boy has the responsibility of fulfilling the commandments, i.e. the Ten Commandments of Exodus chapter 20, and all the other rules for life which have developed from these. At a Bar Mitzvah or Bat Mitzvah ceremony, therefore, the young person involved is publicly accepting that responsibility and will now do his or her best to live according to the Jewish faith.

Following the words with a yod

## Bar Mitzvah

The boy in the photograph, Jacob, is having a rehearsal for his Bar Mitzvah ceremony; he spoke to us about this important occasion and what leads up to it.

'It was my thirteenth birthday last week and, because I am Jewish, I am now Bar Mitzvah – a son of the commandment, but the ceremony to mark this is to be held tomorrow in the synagogue. I have just been practising for the ceremony, and I must confess I am rather excited and not a little nervous! Tomorrow, at the ceremony, I have to read to the congregation from the sacred scroll of our scriptures. The Rabbi (that is, the minister of our synagogue) has been helping me to prepare for this special event. For several years I have attended a class at the synagogue to learn Hebrew, since we read our scriptures in that ancient language; in these classes we also have been taught what it means to live as a Jew and to follow our religion.

'More recently, the Rabbi has been training me to stand up in the synagogue and read aloud from the scriptures; this is what I have been practising. I have also had a test to make sure that I really do know and understand what it means to be a Jew and to live according to Jewish teaching.'

Jacob wore a **tallith** when he was practising for the ceremony. A tallith is a prayer shawl with fringes at either end and these remind the Jew of the commandments of God. When a boy becomes Bar Mitzvah, he wears a tallith in the synagogue services. He also wears a cap, or **yarmulke**, because Jewish men always cover their heads as a mark of respect for the place of worship. Jacob followed the words in the scroll using a small silver pointer, the end of which is shaped as a closed fist with the forefinger in a pointing position. This is called a **yod** and is used partly to protect the scroll and partly as a mark of respect for it as part of the sacred scriptures.

### The Ceremony
Jacob arrived at the synagogue next day for his Bar Mitzvah ceremony looking very smart indeed. He told us that he felt very nervous as he sat near to the Bimah (the raised platform from which he would read) and watched the synagogue filling up with worshippers. He began to wish it was empty, as it had been when he practised!

He was, as you can see, wearing the tallith as at the rehearsal, but also the **tefillin** or phylacteries, one on his left arm and one on his forehead. These are little square boxes with leather straps to hold them in place. Inside are hand-written strips of parchment containing brief passages from the scriptures. From now on, except on the Sabbath, Jacob will wear these at synagogue services as a reminder that he is to concentrate on God's teachings with all his heart and all his mind.

As Jacob sat waiting for the service to begin, many of the worshippers who knew him came and shook him by the hand, wishing him well.

The service started and in the course of it the Ark, where the sacred scrolls are kept, was opened and with great reverence the scroll was carried and laid on the reading desk and unrolled to the passage to be read. Jacob's special moment had come! The Rabbi called out, 'Yakob-ben-Binyamin' which is Hebrew for 'Jacob son of Benjamin'. Jacob made his way forward, climbed the few steps to the Bimah, picked up the yod, found the place in the text and began to read. Although he said he felt very nervous, those listening thought he read with great confidence. When he finished, the men called out, as is the custom, 'Mazal Tov!' which means something like, 'Good Luck!'

In the synagogue service there is the custom of male members of the congregation being 'called to the Torah', i.e. they are invited to stand on the Bimah while the scriptures are being read and, at the appropriate point, to say the words of a blessing. It is regarded as a great honour to be 'called to the Torah'. On the occasion of a Bar Mitzvah it is usual to 'call to the Torah' members of the boy's family, so at Jacob's ceremony his father, grandfather, uncle and brother were all standing beside him on the Bimah.

The Rabbi gave a brief address in which he reminded Jacob, and indeed the rest of the congregation, about the way of life to which he is committed now that he is Bar Mitzvah. After the address, Jacob recited, in Hebrew, the Bar Mitzvah prayer; you can see it on page 45 both in Hebrew and in English.

After the ceremony, the family had a celebration meal with relatives and friends. At this, Jacob was given gifts and good wishes to mark this special day in his life.

We were curious to know what difference this ceremony would make to Jacob. When we asked, we were told:

'There is nothing magical about the ceremony which changes him! However, when a boy has taken part in his Bar Mitzvah ceremony, he feels more committed to live as a Jew; he feels honoured to have been called up to read the scriptures to the congregation, and the congregation now knows him as one who has accepted the responsibilities of his religion. Jewish custom lays down that before a synagogue service can take place, there must be at least ten men present; the boy who is now Bar Mitzvah now counts as one of these ten. There is no guarantee, of course, that a boy who becomes Bar Mitzvah will live according to the Jewish faith all his life, but the ceremony is a memorable occasion to which his mind may turn if he is tempted to stray from practising the faith.'

## Bat Mitzvah

Abigail Cohen is 12 years old. She has attended the classes held at the synagogue to instruct boys and girls in the Jewish faith, and has taken a test, just as Jacob did, to show that she knows and understands what the faith is all about. Now that she has reached her twelfth

# תְּפִלָּה לְיוֹם בַּר מִצְוָה

*Prayer recited by the בַּר מִצְוָה, when called to the Law, before the Blessing ; or after his being addressed by the Minister.*

אָבִי שֶׁבַּשָּׁמַיִם· בְּיוֹם גָּדוֹל וְקָדוֹשׁ זֶה בְּחַיַּי
אָנֹכִי עוֹמֵד לְפָנֶיךָ וְלִפְנֵי הַקָּהָל הַקָּדוֹשׁ הַזֶּה
לְהוֹדִיעַ כִּי גָדַלְתִּי וְהָיִיתִי לְאִישׁ וְכִי מֵהַיּוֹם
עָלַי לְקַיֵּם אֶת־חֻקֵּי תוֹרָתֶךָ אֲשֶׁר יַעֲשֶׂה אוֹתָם
הָאָדָם וָחַי בָּהֶם וּלְהִתְפַּלֵּל אֵלֶיךָ מִדֵּי יוֹם
בְּיוֹמוֹ· בְּרוּחַ נְמוּכָה וּבְלֵב סָמוּךְ אַפִּיל תְּחִנָּתִי
לְפָנֶיךָ כִּי תִתְמְכֵנִי בִּימִין צִדְקֶךָ וְתִתֵּן בְּלִבִּי
לְהָבִין וּלְהַשְׂכִּיל אֶת דְּרָכֶיךָ וּלְהִתְהַלֵּךְ בָּהֶם
כָּל־יְמֵי חַיָּי· בְּרָא לִי לֵב נָכוֹן לְעָבְדְּךָ בְּתָם
לֵבָב לְדָבְקָה בְּאָרְחוֹת צֶדֶק וְיָשָׁר וְלָסוּר מֵרָע
וּמֵהַרְהוּרֵי חֵטְא :

בְּעָמְדִי הַיּוֹם עַל סַף בַּחֲרוּתִי אֲנִי תְפִלָּה:
אָנָּא נְחֵנִי בְחַסְדֶּךָ· חַזְּקֵנִי בְגוּף וּבְנֶפֶשׁ וְאַזְּרֵנִי

Waiting for the service to begin

## BAR MITZVAH PRAYER

*Prayer recited by the Bar Mitzvah, when called to the Law, before the Blessing ; or after his being addressed by the Minister.*

Heavenly Father, at this sacred and solemn hour of my life I stand before thee in the midst of this holy congregation, to declare my duty ever to turn to thee in daily prayer, and to observe the commandments of thy Law by which a man may live worthily. I pray humbly and hopefully before thee to grant me thy gracious help, so that I have the will and the understanding to walk firmly in thy ways all the days of my life. Implant in me a spirit of sincere devotion to thy service, that I may hold fast to what is holy and just and good, and resist all evil and sinful temptations.

As I grow into full manhood, under thy loving care, may bodily strength, mental power and moral courage be developed in me, that I may fulfil my duties to thee with reverence, knowledge and love, as well as my duties to my neighbour, with zeal, sympathy and courtesy.

Today I enter the community, as one worthy to be numbered to form a congregation for public worship, and to assume the full responsibilities of a Jew. Help me, O merciful Father, who hast chosen thy people Israel for thy service, ever to be numbered and known as a faithful son of thy people, zealous for its fair name and proud to share in the burden of the heritage of the congregation of Jacob. Aid my resolve never to separate myself from the community but always to regard myself as a member of the people of Israel, whose welfare and glory it will be my task to maintain and enhance.

May the noble example of our ancestors inspire me always to be ready to sanctify thy Name, and to witness thy protection and care which extend to all thy works. Amen.

_____

birthday she, and several other girls, are to share in the Bat Mitzvah ceremony. She has been present in the synagogue on many occasions when a boy has become Bar Mitzvah and is glad that there is also a ceremony for girls. The occasion

Bat Mitzvah

chosen for the ceremony is an afternoon service at the synagogue on the day following the Sabbath.

The actual Bat Mitzvah ceremony will come towards the end of the service, when the girls come and stand before the congregation and recite together one of the Psalms. Each girl then reads a passage from the scriptures about one of the great Jewish women. Abigail's reading is from the Book of Genesis and it is about Sarah, the wife of Abraham.

After the readings, the girls recite together the **Shema**, that most important statement of Jewish belief, 'Hear O Israel; the Lord our God, the Lord is One'; they also recite the Ten Commandments. The Rabbi then blesses them with the words, 'May he who blessed the mothers of our faith, Sarah, Rebecca, Rachel and Leah, bless these, your daughters, who receive the title, Bat Mitzvah, as a sign of their desire to live a worthy Jewish life.' The girls respond with a prayer, 'Heavenly Father, at this sacred and solemn hour of our lives, we stand before thee and humbly pray that you will help us become faithful daughters of thy people, and to be faithful to thy commandments.'

The Rabbi then gives a brief address in which he encourages the girls to live according to the faith and he gives them good advice to help them in the future. Hebrew Bibles are presented and the girls are congratulated by their friends and members of the family.

Abigail will never have the same responsibilities as Jacob, but the ceremony for her means that she has accepted a commitment to live as a Jewish woman should. One day, perhaps, she, like her mother, will welcome the Sabbath by lighting the Sabbath candles in the home with her daughters and will help to teach her children about the faith.

## Task 1
Describe the special items worn by a Jewish boy at his Bar Mitzvah ceremony and also the items used by him in the ceremony; for each one give a reason why it is thought to be important.

## Task 2
It is the evening before your Bar Mitzvah or Bat Mitzvah ceremony; write a personal prayer which you might pray as you think about the special occasion in which you will be involved on the next day.

## Task 3
Imagine you are looking back on your ceremony and you are describing your recollections of it to someone who belongs to a different faith. Include in your description not only the scene in the synagogue and your part in it but also your feelings about it.

Welcoming the Sabbath

# 8

# Christian

In Christianity there is not one set
ceremony in which a person shows
commitment to the faith; it depends on
which denomination or branch of the
Church is involved, e.g. whether it is the
Church of England, Roman Catholic,
Methodist, United Reformed or Baptist,
etc. The types of ceremonies, however,
fall broadly into two – those usually
known as **Confirmation** and those
involving adult **baptism**. We shall look,
therefore, at Confirmation as it would be
practised in the Church of England and
at baptism as it would be seen as an act
of commitment in a Baptist Church.

## Confirmation

The word 'confirm' means 'to establish
more firmly' and that could describe the
purpose of a ceremony of Confirmation: it
is the hope that the person who wishes to
show commitment to the Christian faith
will become more firmly established as a
follower of Jesus Christ.

At a christening, we have seen how
parents and godparents made promises
on the child's behalf and have said that
they will encourage the child to confirm
these promises when he or she is old
enough to understand what they mean.
There is no set age at which this might
be done: some are ready to declare openly
that they wish to follow the Christian
faith when they are quite young while
others may wait until they are adults.

### Preparation

Libby Harris decided to be confirmed
when she was twelve years old. Her
mother thought she was still rather
young but Libby insisted that she felt
ready to take this important step and
share more fully in the life of the Church.
For three months before the Confirmation
ceremony, Libby attended classes held by
her Vicar so that she could learn more
about what it means to be a Christian.
Libby enjoyed these classes and was glad
of the friendship and company of the
others who also wished to be confirmed.
Together they looked forward eagerly to
the day when the Confirmation would
take place. Libby thought too of her first
Communion which would be an important
part of the occasion.

The Confirmation would take place in
the church which Libby attended but the
service would be taken by the Bishop. A
bishop is an important minister who is
responsible for all the Church of England
churches in a particular area which is
known as a **diocese**. The women and
girls were told that they should wear
white for the ceremony; the fact that
they would all be dressed the same would
show that they were joining together in a
common action; white would symbolise
the purity of their intention.

On the day before her Confirmation,
Libby attended a rehearsal so that she
would know exactly where to sit and
what to do.

The Bishop

## The Service of Confirmation

When Libby was settled in her place in church for the service, she glanced round and saw that the church was crowded, for many relatives and friends of those to be confirmed were present as well as many other members of the congregation. She felt rather nervous when she saw so many faces and thought of going forward towards the altar with them all watching her! 'I should have listened to my mother, after all', she thought; 'she said she thought I was too young!'

The service began when the Bishop entered the church; he looked very splendid wearing the symbols of his office – his long, colourful robes, a hat called a **mitre** and a staff in his hand which looked like a shepherd's crook, known as a **crozier**: this was a reminder that just as a shepherd is to look after his sheep, so the Bishop is to care for the people in his churches.

As Libby joined in the hymns and prayers as the service progressed she began to feel much less nervous. She listened with interest as the Bishop talked to those about to be confirmed reminding them of the way of life to which they were committed. After his address, the Bishop asked the Confirmation candidates to stand and he said to them:

'You have come here to be confirmed. You stand in the presence of God and his Church. With your own mouth and from your own heart you must declare your allegiance to Christ and your rejection of all that is evil. Therefore I ask you these questions: Do you turn to Christ?'

Libby and her friends all said together:
'I turn to Christ.'
'Do you repent of your sins?'
'I repent of my sins.'
'Do you renounce evil?'
'I renounce evil.'

As Libby made these responses she

49

remembered that she had been told how the same questions had been asked of her parents and godparents at her baptism.

There were three other questions which the Bishop asked the candidates and, introducing them, he said:

'You must now declare before God and his Church that you accept the Christian faith into which you were baptised and in which you will live and grow.

Do you believe and trust in God the Father who made the world?

Do you believe and trust in his Son, Jesus Christ, who redeemed mankind?

Do you believe and trust in his Holy Spirit who gives life to the people of God?'

To each of these questions, Libby and the other candidates for Confirmation replied: 'I believe and trust in him.'

After this, the candidates filed out, row by row, to kneel before the Bishop. When Libby's turn came, she knelt before him and felt his hands firmly placed on her head as he said, 'Confirm, O Lord, your servant Elizabeth with your Holy Spirit.' She responded by quietly saying, 'Amen'. Libby returned to her seat and, once all the candidates had been confirmed by the Bishop, said with the whole congregation the prayer:

'Defend, O Lord, your servants with your heavenly grace, that they may continue yours for ever, and daily increase in your Holy Spirit more and more, until they come to your everlasting kingdom.'

Each member of the congregation then turned to his or her neighbour and shook hands, with the greeting: 'The peace of the Lord be always with you.'

'Confirm, O Lord, your servant . . .'

Before Communion a hymn was sung

The Bishop greets those confirmed

## Communion

The final part of the service was Communion. The Bishop spoke about the Last Supper, that occasion when Jesus shared a special meal with his disciples on the night he was arrested. He also reminded them of how Jesus died on the Cross, but rose again from the dead. Libby listened particularly as the Bishop took the bread and said, 'Though we are many, we are one body because we all share the same bread.' Libby felt that she did want to belong to 'this one body', the Church, as she walked forward and knelt at the altar to receive the bread and wine. (See page 54 for more about Communion.)

After the service, the Bishop greeted those who had been confirmed and chatted with them informally. Libby came away feeling what a happy and memorable occasion it had been.

## Task 1

You want to be confirmed, but your parents think you are too young and are not ready for such an important step: what arguments might you give to convince them that you are ready and that you are sincere?

## Task 2

Make a list of the beliefs stated by those being confirmed. What actions in the service express in a symbolic way the beliefs which are held?

## Task 3

Which photograph, in your view, shows the most important part of the service? Describe what is happening and give reasons for your choice.

## Task 4

Here is a photograph of another young girl preparing to leave the house for her Confirmation service. Describe what her thoughts might be as she looks forward to the service.

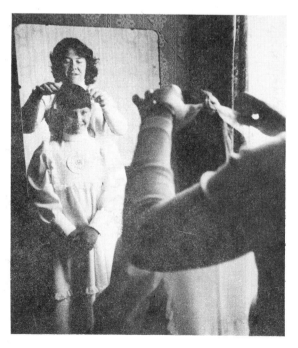

# The Baptism of Believers

When we looked at birth ceremonies practised among Christians, we learned that, while most Christian groups baptise babies, there are some who only have a service of dedication at which the baby is named. These Christian groups believe that baptism is an act which shows commitment to Christ and the Church and is only meaningful when people are old enough to decide for themselves that they want to be Christians and to join the Church.

Very often those who are being baptised in this way are young people in their teens: on the occasion, however, when our photographs were taken, the people being baptised were both elderly. The service took place in one of the Baptist churches in our community.

A Baptist church, instead of having a font which holds only a little water, has a pool set into the floor; this is called a **baptistry** and it holds enough water for the Minister to 'dip' the person being baptised under the water. We talked with the ladies who were baptised at this service and one of them told us:

'As I stepped down into the water, I felt rather nervous but as I stood in the water with the Minister beside me, I began to feel very peaceful. I listened as he said to me, "My sister, do you now confess Jesus Christ as your Saviour and Lord?" I replied, "I do." He then said, "On your confession of faith in Jesus Christ as Saviour and Lord, I baptise you in the name of the Father, the Son and the Holy Spirit." Having said this, he dipped me under the water, and as I was helped out of the baptistry, the congregation were singing the hymn:

"O Jesus I have promised to serve Thee to the end,
Be Thou for ever near me, my Saviour and my friend."'

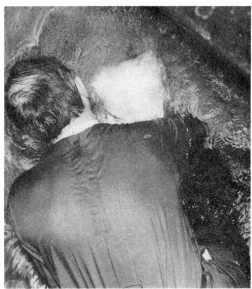

We asked the ladies several questions about the ceremony:

*Our question:* Can you tell us why you decided to be baptised? After all, many people would think it very strange to be dipped in a pool of water, in front of all these people, especially at your age!

*Answer:* Maybe it does seem strange, but the experience for us has been a wonderful one and we both felt this was something we had to do. We have in fact been coming to church for many years and have tried to be good Christians and follow the teaching of Jesus, but we had never actually shown our commitment by joining the Church.

*Our question:* So this baptism has to do with joining the Church?

*Answer:* Yes, it has. We are told in the New Testament that when people believed in Jesus and joined his followers, they were baptised. Baptists believe that this is still an important way to show commitment to Jesus and his Church.

*Our question:* So this ceremony is an initiation into membership of the Church; has the baptism made you Christians?

*Answer:* Oh no! It is simply a way of

showing that we are committed to Christ and the Church. I suppose the water symbolises our belief that Christ has forgiven us and taken away our sins, but it is even more than that. In one of his letters in the New Testament, the Letter to the Romans, chapter 6, Paul the Apostle spoke about 'being baptised into the death of Christ'. 'By baptism', he said, 'we were buried with him' and 'as Christ was raised from the dead, so also we might set our feet upon the new path of life.' So being baptised is a way of symbolising that our old life without Christ is being buried and we rise from the water committed to live a better life with him and with his help. By being baptised we have made a public confession to our faith in Christ: we have declared to all present – 'we are committed to following Christ!' We like very much the photograph on page 55 which shows the wet footprints which we made as we left the baptistry; it seems to remind us of one of the verses of the hymn sung by the congregation at our baptism:

O let me see Thy footmarks,
And in them plant my own;
My hope to follow duly,
Is in Thy strength alone:
O guide me, call me, draw me,
Uphold me to the end;
And then in Heaven receive me,
My Saviour and my Friend.

### Welcomed into Membership
The two ladies, after putting on dry clothes, came back into the service and were welcomed into the membership of the Church as the Minister, on behalf of the Church, gave each of them a firm handshake. The celebration of Communion followed: you will remember that this was also an important part of the service of Confirmation.

# Communion

This act of worship is known by various names depending on which Church is celebrating it. It may be known as Holy Communion, the Mass, the Eucharist, the Lord's Supper or by some other title, but the essential parts of it are the same: bread (or wafer) and wine are used as symbols of the body and blood of Christ, signifying that he gave his life on the Cross so that the world might know more fully about the love of God. The other common feature is that Christians think of taking the bread and wine at Communion as a way of showing, again and again, their commitment to their faith.

### Origins of Communion
Probably the earliest words we have about Communion are those in Paul's first letter to the Corinthians, chapter 11 verses 23 to 26:

> For I received from the Lord what I also delivered to you, that the Lord Jesus on the night when he was betrayed took bread, and when he had given thanks, he broke it, and said, 'This is my body which is for you. Do this in remembrance of me.' In the same way also the cup, after supper, saying, 'This cup is the new covenant in my blood. Do this, as often as you drink it, in remembrance of me.' For as often as you eat this bread and drink the cup, you proclaim the Lord's death until he comes.

Paul was referring to the Last Supper, when Jesus sat down with his disciples on the night he was arrested and shared bread and wine with them.

### Communion – a part of the Commitment Ceremony
As we have seen, Communion forms an important part of the ceremonies of commitment for Christians. In the

photograph on page 55 you can see that the bread and wine is already set out for the Communion which was to follow the baptisms.

In that particular church the bread and wine is taken round the members of the congregation by the deacons (men or women appointed by the church to help the Minister). In many other churches such as the one in which we have seen the service of Confirmation, those taking Communion come out and kneel at the altar and are given the bread with the words, 'The Body of Christ': they are also given the wine, with the words, 'The Blood of Christ'.

## Communion – An Act of Rededication

Although Communion is a part of the Christian ceremonies of commitment, Christians do not just take Communion once; those who take their faith seriously, and try to live according to its teaching, take Communion regularly. In some churches they would have the opportunity to do this every Sunday; in others, it might be once a month or even only once every three months. Every time they take the bread and the wine, however, they remember the death of Christ with thanksgiving and rededicate themselves to go on living as Christians as best as they are able. They remember that their faith has not only to do with worship in church, but it has to do with living according to Christ's teaching in the world outside the church.

*Task 5*

(a) Make a list of the features common to both Confirmation and Believers' Baptism.

(b) Write a brief argument in support of either Confirmation or Believers' Baptism as an important way of marking commitment to the Christian faith.

'The blood of Christ'

*Task 6*

(a) Christian Communion goes back to the Last Supper when Jesus shared bread and wine with his disciples on the night of his arrest. Read the account of this in Mark chapter 14 verses 17 to 26 in your Bible, then write your account of the occasion as if, later, two of the disciples were discussing it; include in it what you think the disciples might have felt about the occasion.

(b) In what ways does the act of Communion make a good way for Christians to rededicate themselves to their faith? Would it, for example, be just as effective to stand up and say, 'I rededicate myself to following Jesus Christ'?

# 9

# Muslim

Most faiths have a ceremony to mark the commitment of the individual believer; Islam, however, has no such specific, once-for-all ceremony of commitment; many Muslims say that every day is like a ceremony of commitment as the individual lives according to his beliefs.

## Five Pillars of Islam

The religion of Islam is likened to a building supported by five pillars; each pillar represents an obligation to be carried out by every Muslim who takes his faith seriously. The five pillars are:
*Faith*
*Prayer*
*Giving to the poor*
*Fasting*
*Pilgrimage.*
  When we looked at birth ceremonies observed by Muslims, we met the Khan family. We talked with Mr Khan about the five pillars and what it means to be a Muslim. He told us that a person can only call himself a Muslim if he is prepared to face up to each of these obligations. The words 'Islam' and 'Muslim' mean 'submission': a true Muslim is one who submits to Allah.

### (1) Faith
A declaration of faith is the first pillar. Muslims refer to this by the Arabic word **Shahadah**. There are various statements of belief which Muslims use in their worship; each of these is called a **Kalimah**. The basic, most important Kalimah looks like this in Arabic, the language of the Muslim scriptures:

and sounds like this in Arabic:

La ilaha illallah
Muhammadu rasulullah

and reads like this in English:

There is no God but Allah
(and) Muhammad is Allah's Messenger.

We were told, 'a person only becomes a Muslim when he has declared this Kalimah.' That set us wondering – do you just have to say these words and you are a Muslim? We were assured that there is much more to it than that! Mr Khan told us, 'Islam consists of belief *and* action; a Muslim is one who holds the belief and who acts accordingly; a Muslim is one who does whatever Allah and his Prophet, Muhammad, through the sacred Qur'an, our scriptures, tells him to do. Faith without action is of no use; faith and action must always go together.'
  We had discovered, therefore, that commitment in Islam means believing in

شعبـان / رمضـان ١٤٠٤ه

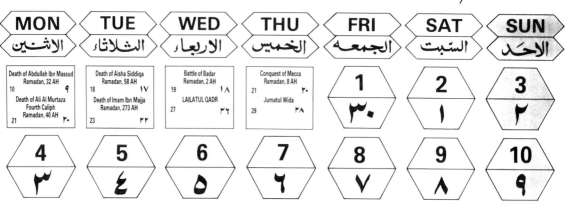

| MON<br>الاثنين | TUE<br>الثلاثاء | WED<br>الاربعاء | THU<br>الخميس | FRI<br>الجمعه | SAT<br>السّبت | SUN<br>الاحَـد |
|---|---|---|---|---|---|---|
| Death of Abdullah Ibn Massud<br>Ramadan, 32 AH<br>10　٩<br>Death of Ali Al Murtaza<br>Fourth Caliph<br>Ramadan, 40 AH<br>21　٢٠ | Death of Aisha Siddiqa<br>Ramadan, 58 AH<br>18　١٧<br>Death of Imam Ibn Majja<br>Ramadan, 273 AH<br>23　٢٢ | Battle of Badar<br>Ramadan, 2 AH<br>19　١٨<br>LAILATUL QADR<br>27　٢٦ | Conquest of Mecca<br>Ramadan, 8 AH<br>21　٢٠<br>Jumatul Wida<br>29　٢٨ | 1<br>٣٠ | 2<br>١ | 3<br>٢ |
| 4<br>٣ | 5<br>٤ | 6<br>٥ | 7<br>٦ | 8<br>٧ | 9<br>٨ | 10<br>٩ |

## Birmingham

| التاريخ<br>Date | الفجر<br>Fajr | الشروق<br>Sunrise | الظهر<br>Zuhr | العصر<br>Asr | المغرب<br>Maghrib | العشاء<br>Isha |
|---|---|---|---|---|---|---|
| 01-03 | 3.18 | 4.49 | 1.11 | 5.11 | 9.25 | 10.28 |
| 04-06 | 3.16 | 4.47 | 1.11 | 5.13 | 9.28 | 10.30 |
| 07-09 | 3.15 | 4.45 | 1.12 | 5.15 | 9.30 | 10.32 |
| 10-12 | 3.13 | 4.44 | 1.12 | 5.16 | 9.33 | 10.35 |
| 13-15 | 3.12 | 4.43 | 1.13 | 5.17 | 9.34 | 10.36 |
| 16-18 | 3.12 | 4.43 | 1.13 | 5.18 | 9.36 | 10.37 |
| 19-21 | 3.12 | 4.43 | 1.14 | 5.19 | 9.37 | 10.38 |
| 22-24 | 3.12 | 4.43 | 1.14 | 5.20 | 9.38 | 10.39 |
| 25-27 | 3.14 | 4.44 | 1.15 | 5.20 | 9.38 | 10.39 |
| 28-30 | 3.15 | 4.46 | 1.16 | 5.21 | 9.38 | 10.40 |

## Bradford

| التاريخ<br>Date | الفجر<br>Fajr | الشروق<br>Sunrise | الظهر<br>Zuhr | العصر<br>Asr | المغرب<br>Maghrib | العشاء<br>Isha |
|---|---|---|---|---|---|---|
| 01-03 | 3.09 | 4.40 | 1.10 | 5.15 | 9.33 | 10.34 |
| 04-06 | 3.07 | 4.38 | 1.11 | 5.17 | 9.36 | 10.37 |
| 07-09 | 3.05 | 4.36 | 1.11 | 5.18 | 9.38 | 10.39 |
| 10-12 | 3.04 | 4.35 | 1.12 | 5.20 | 9.41 | 10.41 |
| 13-15 | 3.03 | 4.34 | 1.12 | 5.21 | 9.42 | 10.42 |
| 16-18 | 3.03 | 4.34 | 1.13 | 5.22 | 9.44 | 10.44 |
| 19-21 | 3.03 | 4.34 | 1.13 | 5.23 | 9.45 | 10.45 |
| 22-24 | 3.03 | 4.34 | 1.14 | 5.24 | 9.46 | 10.46 |
| 25-27 | 3.04 | 4.35 | 1.14 | 5.24 | 9.46 | 10.46 |
| 28-30 | 3.06 | 4.37 | 1.15 | 5.24 | 9.46 | 10.46 |

the one God (of whom Muslims use the Arabic word **Allah**, which means 'God') and acting according to that belief in one's life.

## (2) Prayer

The second pillar of Islam which shows a high degree of commitment is prayer. Five times each day, the call to prayer sounds out from the balcony of the minaret, the tall tower on the mosque. Muslims like Mr Khan respond to this call either by going to the mosque to pray, if possible, or else praying where they are, at home, or even at work. The Arabic word for this prayer rite is **Salat**. This is not just a matter of a hasty sentence, over in a minute, but it involves saying a number of prayers to Allah, and for each one, taking up a different bodily position. (For more detailed information about the prayer rite see the earlier book in this series – *Believers*, pages 82-9.)

On this page is an extract from a calendar for June 1984 which shows the prayer times for two major cities in Britain. The times vary from one month to another since they relate to the time of sunrise and sunset. You will see from the tables that the five prayer times are indicated by Arabic words – Fajr, Zuhr, Asr, Maghrib, Isha.

Minaret at the Birmingham mosque

In the mosque there is usually a board like the one you see here which indicates the prayer times: **Jamat** refers to the worshippers coming together to pray in the mosque for prayers led by the Imam.

The hands of the clock are moved to indicate the times for any particular day. The bottom left-hand clock refers to the Friday service which in a Muslim country is usually at noon, but in Britain may be arranged to suit local circumstances.

Mr Khan told us, 'Prayer helps us to remember Allah and reminds us that we are servants of Allah. Prayer keeps us from evil and helps us to follow the commands of Allah.'

A Muslim should begin offering Salat regularly after he is seven years old; after he is twelve it is compulsory in the sense that he has no right to call himself a Muslim unless he regularly observes Salat.

### (3) Giving to the Poor

This is the third pillar which is known by the Arabic word **Zakat**. You will remember that when the naming ceremony took place for Mr Khan's son, what hair the baby had was shaved off, weighed, and an equivalent sum of money was given to charity. Muslims believe that they have a duty to give to others poorer than themselves, not just on special occasions such as the birth of a baby, but to do so regularly. For this reason, a box marked **Zakat** in Arabic can be seen in the mosque and worshippers put money into this, as they are able, so that poorer people can be helped.

When we asked about Zakat, we were told, 'Commitment to Islam involves not only giving your time for prayer and other religious observances; it also involves giving a share of your money. Islam stands for brotherhood; the Holy Qur'an teaches us that wealth is a trust from Allah and it should be spent as he wants us to spend it. Islam says that all good causes have a claim on our wealth, so we are commanded, if we are reasonably well-off, to pay what we can to help the needy and other good causes. It is a great sin not to share one's wealth with the needy and allow them to suffer from hunger and disease. Muhammad the Prophet even said, "He cannot be a Muslim who eats his fill while his brother is hungry.'"

We were told that the Muslim is expected to work out how much money he requires from his income for daily living, i.e. for food, clothing, housing, etc., for himself and his family; the amount of money he should pay to fulfil his Zakat obligation is then 2½ per cent of what is left.

Giving money, therefore, is another way in which a Muslim shows commitment to his faith.

### (4) Fasting
The Arabic word for this fourth pillar of Islam is **Sawm**. The Muslim fasts from dawn to dusk every day during the ninth month of the Muslim calendar, the month of **Ramadan**. (The Muslim calendar is worked out according to the phases of the moon and not the sun, so the Muslim year is slightly shorter than a year as we know it in the West. Ramadan, therefore, comes at a different time in our calendar each year.) This fasting means not only going without food but also without drink.

If you look at the calendar extract on page 58 you will see that in 1984, Ramadan started on June 2nd: study the tables below the calendar and you will see the times of sunrise; sunset is a little before the time shown for Maghrib. These times bring home to us how demanding the Ramadan fast is for the Muslim.

Islam teaches that if a Muslim strictly observes the fast but is not careful about his behaviour then his fast is of no value. Almost certainly someone will ask, 'If you are a Muslim and do not fast, what will happen to you?' Muslims say that in Salat (prayer) and Zakat (giving to the poor), their actions can be seen by others; however, when it comes to fasting, it is obviously easy to cheat. Mr Khan said,

'There is nothing to stop one going off on one's own and eating something, while pretending to keep the fast; no one would know, but Allah would know! That is part of the purpose of fasting: since we are aware that Allah knows we are fasting, it makes us remember him and it makes us obedient to him for we believe he has told us to fast. It also strengthens our character and helps us learn self-control, for it is not easy to fast; we are always aware of the temptation to eat and drink! The Ramadan fast also gives us a strong sense of unity with fellow Muslims all over the world who are also fasting; in addition it allows us to remember, each year, what it is like to be hungry and so we are, in a small way, sharing the suffering of people who never have enough to eat.'

We asked Mr Khan, 'What about boys and girls – are they expected to fast?' The answer we were given was, 'When boys and girls reach the age of 12 they are expected to fast, like all other Muslims, during the month of Ramadan. Fasting during Ramadan is like prayer; if you do not observe it after the age of 12 you have no right to call yourself a Muslim.'

### (5) Pilgrimage
The final pillar of Islam is known by the Arabic word **Hajj** which means 'pilgrimage'. Every Muslim has a duty, if at all possible, to make a journey at least once in his lifetime to Mecca, which is in the country we now know as Saudi Arabia. Mecca is special to Muslims for two reasons: firstly, the Prophet Muhammad was born there and secondly, there is a cube-shaped building there known as the **Kaaba**; this is very sacred indeed to Muslims, who say that it is the 'House of Allah'. When telling us about this, Mr Khan added, 'not that Allah needs a house and he does not live in any one place, but we need a place to which we can travel to worship him in a special

Pilgrims at the Kaaba (right)

way and we also need a place which is a centre to which Muslims throughout the world can turn their attention'.

We asked, 'What if you are poor and cannot afford to go to Mecca?' The answer was, 'You only make the pilgrimage if your circumstances will allow you to do so. If by making the journey you have to neglect your family and deprive them in any way, it would be quite wrong to do so.'

After thinking about these five pillars of Islam we were certainly aware that, although there is no specific ceremony of commitment, there is no doubt that the demands which the faith makes on a devout Muslim are very considerable.

*Task 1*
On this page is a photograph of the Birmingham Mosque. Draw the front of a mosque similar to this, but design it in such a way that it provides a reminder of the five pillars of Islam. Name each one of them.

*Task 2*
At what age do you think a Muslim is

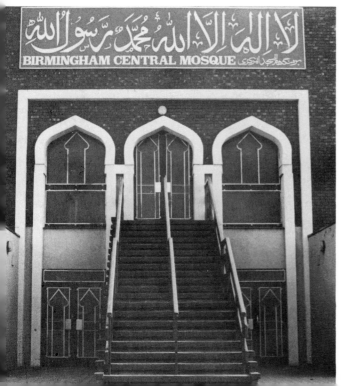

regarded as being old enough to show full commitment to his faith? Which rules would be most difficult for a person of that age? Give reasons for your answer.

*Task 3*
Imagine you are a Muslim living in Britain; write an account of a typical day in your life during the month of Ramadan. Remember to include the times of your prayers; also describe how you feel at different times of the day about your fast. What do you believe is the purpose of your fasting and how does it show your commitment?

*Task 4*
There is a story of a Muslim in Persia, many years ago, who saved for a long time so that he could go on pilgrimage to Mecca. At last he was able to set out with a few friends. One day, on the journey, he met a woman who was very poor indeed and he felt so sorry for her that he gave her food and money. By doing this, however, he could no longer afford to continue on the journey to Mecca. He made the excuse to his friends that he was unwell and would follow later; in fact, he sadly returned home.

When his friends returned, they congratulated him on making the pilgrimage! He explained that he had not been to Mecca at all, but his friends only smiled and said that they had seen him many times, and, in a vision, Allah had told them that he had made a wonderful pilgrimage and that Allah was well-pleased with him!

(a) What does this old Muslim legend suggest about the pillar of Islam which might be regarded as most important?

(b) All five pillars of Islam are very important; show briefly how they are all related to each other and all have to do with commitment to Allah and to the Muslim way of life.

# 0

# Sikh

f you have studied the Sikh birth
ceremony described in Part I you will
remember that at the naming ceremony
a child is given a taste of a mixture of
sugar and water known as **Amrit**. Later
in life, when a Sikh decides to become a
fully committed member of the Sikh
brotherhood, known as the **Khalsa**,
Amrit again plays an important part;
indeed the ceremony is often referred to
as The Amrit Ceremony.

## The Amrit Ceremony

### Origins
The Sikh faith was founded by Guru
Nanak, and after his death the Sikhs
were led by a succession of nine other
Gurus, the last of whom was Guru Gobind
Singh. (He declared that on his death the
sacred writings would be their teacher;
this came to be known as the Guru
Granth Sahib, which means, 'Lord Teacher
Book'.)

In the year 1699 Guru Gobind Singh
summoned the Sikhs to Anandpur in the
Punjab to celebrate the New Year festival
of Baisakhi. He was particularly anxious
to have as many present as possible for it
was a difficult time for Sikhs; many were
persecuted and were tempted to give up
their faith. Thousands gathered around a
tent which had been erected and waited
to listen to the Guru's words.

When Guru Gobind appeared he was
fully armed; he stood on a platform and,
instead of the words of blessing they
expected to hear, he made a very strange
request. He asked who would give his
head as proof of his faith. There was a
hush in the shocked crowd until one
man, Daya Ram, came forward. The
Guru took him into the tent and re-
emerged with a blood-stained sword.
Once again he made the same request;
although the people were convinced that
he had killed Daya Ram, a second brave
man, Dharam Dass, stepped forward to
volunteer his life for the Guru. When
Guru Gobind re-appeared once again
with the blood-stained sword, many
people were afraid and left the scene
quietly. Others ran to tell the Guru's
mother that he had gone mad!

The Guru continued to make his awful
request until, in all, five men had gone
into the tent to give their lives for their
faith. When Guru Gobind went into the
tent with the fifth man, Himmab Rai, he
remained there for a long time; when he
came out of the tent there was a gasp of
relief from the crowd; following him were
the five volunteers dressed like the Guru
and carrying swords and all perfectly
well! What had happened in the tent?
Only the Guru and his five volunteers
knew, but the crowds realised that they
had seen the sort of followers the Guru
wanted – brave and loyal to their faith to
the extent that they would be willing to
give their lives.

The crowds raised the cry, 'Sat Sri
Akal' meaning, 'God is truth'. The Guru

called the five his **panj pyares** and declared them to be the foundation of the Sikh brotherhood which he called the Khalsa which means 'the Pure Ones'. He then took a steel bowl and filled it with water: his wife added sugar pellets and the Guru stirred the mixture with a **Khanda**, a short, double-edged sword; he recited five prayers as he stirred. He baptised his five 'Pure Ones' by giving them the Amrit mixture to drink and also sprinkling some of it on their heads and their eyes. He said that from now on all males should take the name Singh, meaning 'lion', for this indicated the courage he demanded from his Khalsa; in the same way women were to be called Kaur, meaning 'princess': in giving them all a common name he unified them in one brotherhood. The Guru then gave the Khalsa a code of conduct by which to live.

This baptism introduced by Guru Gobind created a community of united, righteous men who would fight for justice and freedom against those who would oppress them and take away the liberties of others.

The members of the Khalsa were ordered to wear five articles, each of which, in Punjabi, begins with the letter 'K'; these from now on would distinguish them as Sikhs and mark them out as men prepared to fight for truth.

The five 'Ks' are:

*Kesh* – long hair, a symbol of devotion to God.
*Kara* – a steel bracelet worn on the right wrist to remind a Sikh of his unity with God and the Khalsa.
*Kanga* – a comb: Sikhs must keep their long hair tidy and in place. This is a symbol of discipline.
*Kirpan* – a sword symbolising a willingness to fight for justice.
*Kaachs* – shorts worn to symbolise moral purity.

Preparing for the Amrit ceremony

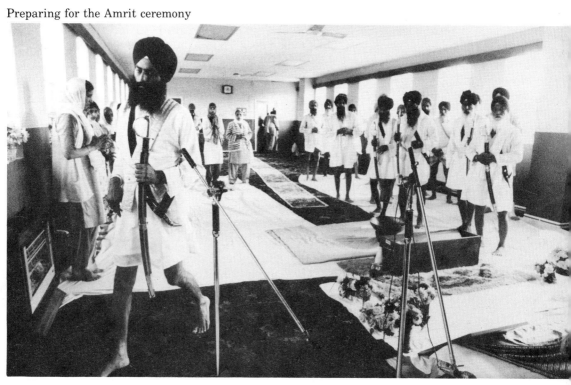

## The Amrit Ceremony Today

A Sikh baptism is conducted with great ceremony and in an atmosphere of dedication and solemnity. On the occasion we attended, forty people were to be baptised at the end of the normal morning service in the gurdwara. All morning the excitement had been building up; crowds had attended the worship and many people stopped to glance into the room set aside for the baptisms, but no one was allowed to enter.

The Guru Granth Sahib was covered since it was not being read. In front of the holy book were the articles required for the ceremony – a steel bowl, sugar pellets, a double-edged sword called a Khanda and, on one side, the Karah Parshad in a covered bowl.

The initiates, i.e. those to be baptised, arrived dressed in clean clothes, having taken a bath and washed their hair in readiness for the ceremony. All wore the five Ks, the symbols of Sikhism. Their ages ranged from sixteen to sixty, since anyone over sixteen can receive baptism, provided he or she is prepared to live a disciplined life.

They filed into the room and were followed by five Sikh men called by the same title as that given to the five who were willing to be killed by Guru Gobind Singh – 'the Panj Pyares', i.e. 'the five beloved'. These are men given the responsibility of conducting baptisms. Only men who are known to be living a true Sikh life and who are already baptised members of the Khalsa are allowed to baptise. These five were dressed in white clothing with blue sashes and each wore a sword. They had a very important duty to fulfil for, during the ceremony, as well as baptising the initiates, they would give them the advice and help needed to live the life of a Khalsa Sikh.

## Preparing the Amrit

The initiates stood in the presence of the Granth and promised to dedicate their lives to the teaching of the Ten Gurus and to the Sikh community. The Panj Pyares gathered around a steel bowl known as a **Karah** and a prayer was offered asking for God's help in the ceremony.

The steel bowl is important for in it the Amrit used for baptism will be prepared. The Granthi read a hymn from the holy book; this hymn was chosen at random and in this way they showed their belief that the Granth is a book of guidance. The Granthi waved a chauri over the book as he read.

After this reading the Panj Pyares poured water and sugar pellets into the bowl and all five sat around it with the right knee on the floor and the left raised. This position resembles that which an archer takes up before firing an arrow from a bow. All five placed their hands on the bowl and recitations from the Granth began which were to last for almost two hours!

Each of the Panj Pyares took a turn to recite from memory some of the Sikh prayers, and, as he did so, he stirred the Amrit mixture with the double-edged sword. These prayers included the Japji, important words composed by Guru Nanak, and prayers by others of the Ten Gurus. They sum up what the Sikh faith is all about, e.g. one of them says:

'God has no marks or symbols,
He is of no colour, of no caste,
He is not even of any lineage,
His form, hue, shape and garb
Cannot be described by anyone;
He is immovable, self-existent,
He shines in his own splendour,
No one can measure his might.'

The Panj Pyares stood and held the bowl up so that everyone could see it; as they did so they said a prayer of thanksgiving and requested the blessings of God on those who were to receive baptism.

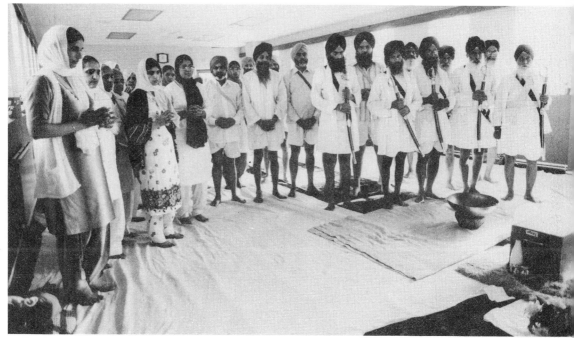
The initiates and the Panj Pyares

## Receiving the Amrit

Each individual came forward and knelt in the position previously adopted by the Panj Pyares. The Amrit was given five times to them in their cupped hands for them to drink; also five times it was sprinkled on their eyes and five times on their heads. Each time the Amrit was received, the initiates repeated:

'Waheguru ji ka Khalsa,
Waheguru ji ki fateh.'

This can be translated as:

'The Khalsa is dedicated to God,
The victory belongs to God alone.'

When a Sikh drinks the Amrit he shows that he will not in future eat or drink anything which has been gained by evil means; when it is sprinkled on his eyes it means that from this day onwards he will not look at evil things; sprinkling Amrit on the head symbolises the desire that the person will grow in greater understanding of the Sikh faith.

The baptised Sikhs gathered in a semi-circle and they drank the remaining Amrit as the bowl was passed from one to another; drinking from the same bowl shows that they wish to live as brothers according to the teaching contained in the Granth.

## The Duties of True Sikhs

An important sacred poem from the Granth known as the **Mool Mantra** gives some basic Sikh beliefs about God:

'There is one God,
Eternal truth is his name:
Creator of all things
Fearing nothing and at enmity with nothing,
Timeless is his image;
Not begotten, being of his own being:
By the grace of the Guru, made known to men.'

his statement was recited five times by ꞏe Panj Pyares and by the initiates. The ꞏnior member of the five Panj Pyares, as representative of the Khalsa, then told ꞏe initiates of their duties.

The baptised Sikhs must remember to ꞏve by the teaching of the Gurus; they ꞏust pray daily – in the morning, after ꞏnset, and before going to bed; the five ꞏs must be worn; intoxicating drink of ꞏny kind must be avoided; they must not ꞏerform any ceremony which goes against ꞏikh principles.

Other important matters which were ꞏressed were: Sikhs must not cut their ꞏair; they must not smoke tobacco; they ꞏust be faithful in marriage. Should any ꞏf these rules be broken, then the person ꞏould be regarded as having lapsed from ꞏe Sikh faith, since he had failed to ꞏlfil his religious duties.

The memorable ceremony ended with ꞏe Ardas, the final prayer in an act of ꞏikh worship, and then the newly baptised ꞏikhs received a portion of Karah ꞏarshad.

# The Turban

The turban is not one of the five Ks and yet Sikhs consider that wearing a turban is important. There have sometimes been difficulties for the Sikh community when they have persisted in wearing the turban in this country; one example was the time when Sikhs who had motor cycles refused to wear crash helmets since this would mean that they had to remove the turban. They were so determined that they fought this ruling and won the right to ride a motor cycle with only the turban for protection.

When Kulbinder was eleven years old his parents decided he was old enough to wear a turban. Mr and Mrs Bhamra invited many relatives and friends to their home for this special occasion. The Granth was brought to their home from the gurdwara with great ceremony and care was taken to ensure that it remained at a higher level than the people who carried it. Two days before Kulbinder received his turban, a continuous reading

ꞏarrying the Granth

Putting on the turban

of the Granth began at his home; men who were trained to read the Granth correctly, spent two hours each reading aloud the words of the holy book; this reading went on day and night for forty-eight hours until the whole Granth had been read. On the day of its completion, musicians were invited to the home and everyone listened to their songs. Kulbinder sat at the front of the room. He was shown how to put on the turban; this is quite a difficult task for an eleven year old, for the turban consists of a piece of material five metres long!

When it was on his head securely, Kulbinder sat down and was given a garland from his father. Everyone congratulated him and came forward to give him gifts of money.

Kulbinder is now fourteen years old and is an expert at putting on his turban which, as a true Sikh, he hopes to wear for the rest of his life.

We asked Kulbinder, 'Why is it so important to wear a turban?' He told us that the Gurus all wore turbans and they commanded the Sikhs to be like them and follow their example. Sikhs want to show that they are united and one of the ways in which they can do this is by all wearing a turban; it also serves as a badge by which their faith can be displaye to the world.

This turban ceremony for Kulbinder was one in which he showed commitmen to his faith; later he would hope to comm himself more fully to the Sikh brotherhoo in an Amrit ceremony.

The occasion is marked with gifts

## Task 1

Describe the first Amrit ceremony which took place in 1699. In your account explain why you think the Guru acted as he did and why he gave certain rules by which the members of the brotherhood should live.

## Task 2

(a) Describe how the following are used in the ceremony: Khanda, Karah, Amrit.

(b) What rules is a baptised Sikh expected to obey? Which of the rules, in your opinion, would be most difficult to follow?

## Task 3

Kulbinder wears a turban as a symbol of his commitment; what other symbols will he wear after he becomes a member of the Sikh brotherhood? Do you think the wearing of such symbols is likely to strengthen the faith of the person who wears them? Give reasons for your answer.

## Task 4

Look carefully at the photographs in this section and describe

(a) how the room is prepared for the Amrit ceremony, and

(b) the dress of the Panj Pyares, explaining why they are dressed in this way.

## Additional Tasks on Ceremonies of Commitment

1 In the ceremonies of commitment you have studied, the age of people involved has varied considerably. The law in Britain says that you can drive a car when you are seventeen and vote at eighteen; is there, in your opinion, a 'best' age at which people might be encouraged to commit themselves to a religious faith? Give reasons for your answer.

2 Is a ceremony to mark commitment to a faith important in your view? What purpose might it serve (a) to the individual involved, and (b) to the faith community to which he or she belongs?

3 Commitment to a faith should 'show' in the lives of those who are committed. Choose two of the faiths you have studied and describe how you would expect commitment to be seen in the lives of followers of each faith.

4 When followers of a faith go to live in a country in which a different religion from their own has shaped the community's way of life, it may be more difficult to carry out the teaching of that faith: e.g. a Muslim living in Britain may find it difficult to observe all the five prayer times. Consider such difficulties in relation to several of the faiths you have studied, including those of a Christian living in a non-Christian country. Do you consider it important that people who have a religious commitment should carry out the teaching of their faith regardless of where they are living?

# Part III
# Marriage Ceremonies
# 11
# Hindu

The Hindu bride

Hindus have long believed that marriage is for life and that a secure family home is very important; indeed, one of the Hindu holy books, the Rig Veda, states, 'Bride and bridegroom never be disunited: be happy in your home.' Marriage is, therefore, regarded as so important a step to take that it is traditionally arranged by the family. When a boy or girl reaches marriageable age, senior members of the family begin to look for a suitable partner. They look for a person who has a similar education, background and temperament and one whom they consider will make their child happy. When a suitable person has been found, the couple are introduced. Both have the right to refuse to marry and if this happens the negotiations begin again.

## Before the Marriage

Prem and Shobha are Hindus whose marriage was arranged by their families. When Shobha was eighteen and had completed her education and Prem was twenty-four and was studying for his PhD degree at university, they were legally married in a Registry Office; this was to satisfy the law in Britain. This stage, for them, was only a formality; only the religious service would make

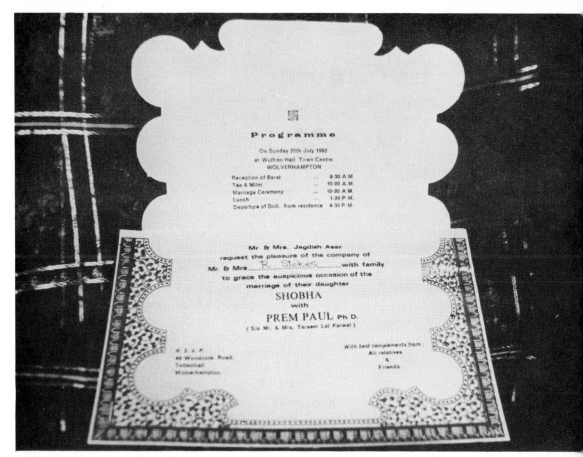

them man and wife in the eyes of the Hindu community and this was not to occur until a year later! During this year they continued to live separately and saw very little of each other. July 25th was the date set for the wedding ceremony; Mrs Asar, Shobha's mother, had many preparations to make, but finally all was arranged and the invitations were sent out to friends and relatives.

## The Wedding

On the day of the wedding, Shobha left home very early with her sisters and friends to travel to the hall which had been booked for the ceremony. She was dressed, as is traditional, in a red sari for her wedding; she also wore many items of gold which had been given her as gifts from her family.

The large hall was beautifully decorated one part had been arranged so that the guests could be entertained with tea and food as they arrived, the other part was prepared for the religious ceremony. At the front was the shrine at which the marriage was to take place. This was a large structure consisting of four pillars which held up a covering to form a canopy. It was draped with material and decorations and on the top the names 'Prem' and 'Shobha' were written in large letters.

News quickly spread through the assembled guests that the bridegroom had arrived and everyone hurried outside to greet him and his party. Prem's face was completely hidden by a decorative overing attached to his turban. At one time, a bride and bridegroom would have seen each other's faces for the first time only when a veil held between them during the ceremony was lowered. In the case of Prem and Shobha, they had of course met and approved of each other, but Prem's face covering was a reminder of this old custom. The women greeted the bridegroom by singing traditional songs and placing garlands of flowers around his neck.

Prem walked to the shrine to join his bride and they sat together. Prem was offered water and a mixture of yoghurt and honey; this symbolises hospitality and expresses the hope that life will be pleasant for the couple in the years ahead.

By now, the guests had taken their places and the close relatives sat round the shrine. Mr and Mrs Asar sat by Shobha, and Prem's family sat on the other side by their son. Mr Asar, Shobha's father, placed her right hand into the bridegroom's right hand to show that he was willing to give his daughter to Prem.

In the photograph you can see a container in front of the bride and bridegroom; this was for the sacred fire which is very important in the marriage ceremony. Since marriage is a Samskara, i.e. a religious act or ritual which marks an important stage in life, a priest was present to conduct the ceremony. Throughout the ceremony the priest read in Sanskrit, an ancient religious language, and generally directed the proceedings. Prem and Shobha followed his instructions but did not speak to each other.

Hands of bride and bridegroom joined

## Joining the Bride and Bridegroom

The sacred fire was kindled by the priest placing sticks in the container; Mr Asar added crushed incense and the bridegroom poured ghee over the sticks, and the fire burned brighly.

The sacred fire (above)

Some of the statements the priest read at this point were, 'You are my wife . . . remain supported and nourished by me . . . God bless this my wife with offspring. Prem and Shobha were symbolically joined together by a piece of material from Shobha's sari being tied to the scarf which Prem wore; joined together in this way they walked round the fire while the priest said, 'You and I accept each other with understanding and complete love. You are like soil and I am like the sun; come, let us marry and have children.' When they had circled the floor, Shobha placed her foot on a stone and the priest said, 'Ascend this stone and be as firm as a rock': this is to symbolise the fact that after marriage Shobha is expected to be loyal to Prem and his family.

Shobha's male cousins poured rice into her hands and she put it into her husband's hand. In the photograph on page 75, Prem is offering this rice to the fire. This process was repeated four times while the priest read the words, 'This girl in leaving her parents and joining her husband's family has accepted his way of life.' Just as rice flourishes and grows when it is planted in new soil, so the

Bride's sari tied to bridegroom's scarf

Rice offered to the fire

'Take the first step for the sake of food,
Take the second for strength,
Take the third for wealth,
Take the fourth for happiness,
Take the fifth for children,
Take the sixth for sustenance,
Take the seventh for unity.'

Prem and Shobha completed their seven steps round the blazing fire and were now man and wife. They placed a hand near each other's hearts while the priest said, 'I put your heart into my vows. Let my mind be in accordance with your mind; let God join you with me.'

The couple were offered some sweet foods as guests came forward to bless them and give them gifts of money; they were also showered with rose petals. As Prem removed the decorative covering which had veiled his face the guests said, 'Let the life of the newly married couple be happy and prosperous; let fortune attend you.'

So Prem and Shobha were married in the traditional Hindu way and had observed the rites of their religion. Shobha has accepted that from now on she is part of her husband's family. She has entered a new status and stage of her life as a wife and will be expected to assume her religious duties as well as her wifely duties in the home. These religious duties include such things as saying prayers before the family shrine in the home, offering food before the statues of the gods and later sharing this food with the family which is now regarded as holy or prashad, since it has been offered to the gods. Eventually, when she has children, it will also be her duty to teach them about the family religion. Prem, too, in the ceremony has accepted his new responsibility of being a good husband to Shobha and being loyal and faithful to her.

hope is being expressed that Shobha's new life with Prem will be happy and successful.

When the couple were seated again, Prem placed red dye on Shobha's hair and the priest declared that her state of being single had come to an end: she must now consider herself a married woman.

### The Seven Steps

The highlight of the whole ceremony was the taking of seven steps round the sacred fire. More ghee was put on it to make it blaze up; the bride and groom stood and as they took each step they paused to hear the words of each of seven vows repeated. The seven vows were:

Guests bless the couple

## Task 1
Look carefully at the photographs in this section to help you with the following:

(a) Describe how the bride and bridegroom were dressed.

(b) Make a copy of the invitation and design your own cover.

(c) Write a list of the main features of a Hindu wedding.

## Task 2
(a) What words and actions in the ceremony express the idea that the couple are to remain faithful for the rest of their lives?

(b) Choose two of the symbolic acts in the service and explain what they mean.

## Task 3
It appears that in taking seven steps round the sacred fire, hopes are being expressed about what their future life may be like. Describe what these hopes are. How important do you think each of them is? If you were told you could choose any two of these, say with reasons which you would choose.

## Task 4
Many Hindus say, 'In the West you fall in love and marry; we Hindus marry and then fall in love!' What steps were taken before the marriage and during the ceremony to try to ensure that the couple have every opportunity to fall in love once they are married?

# 12
# Jewish

There is a saying among Jews that 'Jewish marriages do not take place on Sabbaths or festivals since by mixing joyous events one would miss out on joy by celebrating two joyful events on the same day!'

The Chuppah

As a Jewish bride enters the synagogue with her father and bridesmaid she can see ahead of her a canopy placed in front of the Bimah, i.e. the place from which the scriptures are read in a synagogue service. This canopy is known as a **Chuppah** and a Jewish wedding always takes place with the bride and bridegroom standing under such a canopy.

Explanations about this custom seem to vary but most Jews see it as a symbol of the new home and the man and woman who are in love being united under one roof. It is also said that the Chuppah is closed on top to suggest the privacy in which the husband and wife can enjoy each other's company, but it is open on all sides to remind them that they are also part of a community and should not exclude their friends from the happiness of their home.

## The Ceremony

In the ceremony which we witnessed the bride and groom took up their places under the Chuppah and the Rabbi began by reading some sentences from the scriptures:

'Blessed be he who comes in the name of the Lord:
We bless you from the House of the Lord.
Serve the Lord with joy; come before him with gladness.'

He went on to chant:

'He who is mighty, blessed and great above all beings, may he bless the bridegroom and the bride.'

After this he gave a short address in which he reminded the couple of the serious responsibilities of marriage and gave them some good advice for the beginning of their life together.

## The First Cup of Wine
After the address the Rabbi took a cup of wine and, before giving it to the bridegroom and the bride to drink, he held it up saying the words of the blessing:

'Blessed art thou O Lord our God, King of the Universe, who createst the fruit of the vine.'

He followed this with the words of another blessing:

'Blessed art thou O Lord our God, King of the Universe, who hast sanctified us by thy commandments . . . Blessed art

thou, O Lord our God, who sanctifies thy people Israel by the rite of the canopy and the sacred covenant of wedlock.

## The Ring
The most important part of the whole ceremony came next. The Rabbi took the bride's left hand and held it up so that the bridegroom could place the wedding ring on her finger; as he did so, the bridegroom said, 'Behold, you are consecrated to me by this ring according to the Law of Moses and of Israel.' (In some synagogues the bride and bridegroom will also exchange vows.)

In many Jewish communities the ring is placed on the forefinger of the bride's right hand; they say that this is the finger with which she points and it will clearly be seen that she is married! Some who favour the left hand say that from the fourth finger of the left hand, a vein goes direct to the heart!

באחד בשבת בששה ימים לחדש יסחו שנת חמשת אלפי"ם ישבע מאי"
ושלשים ושתים לבריאת העולם לפניני שאנו מנין כאן במתא בי"ט ני"ם
ניו יורק באמריקה הצפונה איך החתן נדליה זרח בר צבי המכני"
קרדיטור אמר לה להדא בתולתא אסתר ריבה בת וילף לב הכהן הכסמא
אזיגברג הוי לי לאנתו כדת משה וישראל ואנא אפלח יוקי"ר איד עזי"ם
יתיכי ליכי כהלכות עוברין יהודאין דפלחין ומקרין יזני וסמפרנסין לנשי"ד"ין
בקישטא ויהיבנא ליכי מהר בתוליכי כסף זוז די"ד מאתי דחזי ליכי מדאו'י"תא
יסדוני' וכסותיכי סמקובכי ומיעל לותיכי כאורח כל ארעא וצביאת מרת אסתר ריבה
בתולתא דא יהות לה לאנתו ודן נדוניא דהנעלת ליה מבי אבוה בי"ן בכסף ב"ן
בדהב בין בתכשיטין במאני דלבושא בשמושי דירה ובשמושי דערסא ומקבל עלי"
נדליה זרח חתן דני' במאה וזקוקים כסף צריף וצבי נדליה זרח חתי דן ותוסיף"ך
לה מן דיליה עוד מאה וזקוקים כסף צרוף אחרים כנגדן סך הכל מאתין זקוקים
כסף צרוף וכך אמר נדליה זרח חתי דני אחריות שטר כתובתא דא נדונאד"ין
ותוספתא דא קבלית עלי ועל ירחי בתראי להתפרע מכל שפר ארג
נכסין וקנינין דאית לי תחות כל שמיא דקנא"י ודעתיד" דצבא"
למקנא נכסין דאית ראית להון אחריות ודלי"
להון אחריות כלהון יהון אחו"־־איך

יע־בא"י לפ"ריע מנדהי שט"ר
כתובתא דא נדניא די" יתסע"ת
דא מנא ואפלי מן נ"ל־בא
דעל מתא"אי בחיי ובתר חיי
מי־ימא דני זלעלם ואחרית
שטר כתובתא דא נדניא
דין וזסטפתא דא קבל
עלי־נדליה זרח חתן דנ
כחומר כל שטרי כתובות
ותוספתות דנהגן בבנית
ישראל העשויין כ־רתקן
חכמינו זכרונם לברכה דלא
כאסמכתא ידלא כטופסי דשטרי
וקנינא מן נדליה זרח בר צבי המכנה קרדיטור
חתן דני למרת אסתר ריבה בת וילף לב הכהן המכונה אזענ־־ג
בתולתא דא על כל מה דכתוב ומפורש לעיל במנא דכשר למקנא ביה יהכל שריר יד
קאום        עד        עד        עד

## The Ketubah

The next important part of the ceremony involved the reading of a document. It is the custom among Jews for a marriage contract to be drawn up: this is known as a **Ketubah** and sets out the willingness of the bridegroom and the bride to enter into this marriage; it also reminds both of them of their responsibilities as husband and wife. In many Jewish weddings it is signed by the bridegroom before the bride enters the synagogue; only when it is signed is the signal given for her to enter. On this page you can see an example of this important document; some contracts are entirely in Hebrew, others are in Hebrew with an English translation.

Following the custom, the Ketubah was read aloud to the congregation at the wedding at which we were present, and it was then signed by the bride and by two witnesses and by the Rabbi who conducted the ceremony.

Signing the Ketubah

Other interesting views expressed by Jews about the ring are:

'It must be smooth, with no decoration on it, to ensure a smooth, unbroken married life.'

'A ring has no beginning and no ending, so may the love of the bride and groom never come to an end.'

'Rings which are joined together form a chain; the wedding ring, therefore, symbolises the new link which this couple adds to the long chain of generations of Jews stretching back to the time of Abraham, father of the Jewish people, and his wife, Sarah.'

## Seven Blessings and the Second Cup of Wine

At this point in the ceremony, the Rabbi blessed the couple by reciting in Hebrew the words of seven blessings:

Blessed art thou, O Lord our God, King of the universe, who createst the fruit of the vine.

Blessed art thou, O Lord our God, King of the universe, who hast created all things to thy glory.

Blessed art thou, O Lord our God, King of the universe, Creator of man.

Blessed art thou, O Lord our God, King of the universe, who hast made man in thine image, after thy likeness, and hast prepared unto him, out of his very self, a perpetual fabric. Blessed art thou, O Lord, Creator of man.

May she who was barren (Zion) be exceeding glad and exult, when her children are gathered within her in joy. Blessed art thou, O Lord, who makest Zion joyful through her children.

O make these loved companions greatly to rejoice, even as of old thou didst gladden thy creature in the garden of Eden. Blessed art thou, O Lord, who makest bridegroom and bride to rejoice.

Blessed art thou, O Lord our God, King of the universe, who hast created joy and gladness, bridegroom and bride, mirth and exultation, pleasure and delight, love, brotherhood, peace and fellowship. Soon O Lord, our God, may there be heard in the cities of Judah, and in the streets of Jerusalem, the voice of joy and gladness, the voice of the bridegroom and the voice of the bride, the jubilant voice of bridegrooms from their canopies, and of youths from their feasts of song. Blessed art thou, O Lord, who makest the bridegroom to rejoice with the bride.

When the Rabbi had recited all of these, he again took the cup of wine and gave it to both the bridegroom and the bride to drink. It is said that there are seven blessings because according to the story in the Book of Genesis the Creation of the world took seven days; marriage is compared to creation – from a marriage new life will be created. One ancient Jewish writing says, 'Since Creation, God has been engaged in matchmaking!' (i.e. in making marriages.)

81

## Smashing the Wine Glass

After these blessings came a very strange part of the ceremony: a wine glass was taken, wrapped in tissue paper to prevent bits of glass being scattered around, and crushed by the bridegroom's heel!

Apparently at one time the glass would have been thrown against the wall by the bridegroom! Explanations for this strange custom vary: many say that it is a reminder of the destruction of the Jerusalem Temple in 70 CE and that even in the midst of such a joyous occasion as a wedding, they should pause for a moment to remember the sorrows and the hardships in the history of their people. Others say that, 'as one step shatters the glass, so one act of unfaithfulness will destroy the holiness and happiness of the home.'

With this strange but significant act the wedding ceremony ended, and, as the bride and groom came out together from under the Chuppah, the congregation called out in Hebrew, 'Mazal Tov! Mazal Tov!' which means, 'Good luck! Best wishes!'

As is the custom at most marriages, the couple and their guests went to a reception at which they had a meal, and toasts were drunk to wish the happy couple well and speeches made in which many good wishes were expressed.

*Task 1*
Describe in your own words a Jewish wedding for the benefit of a friend who knows nothing about what takes place.
*or*
Write the script for a radio commentary on a Jewish wedding.

*Task 2*
Important symbols in a Jewish wedding are:
(i) standing under the Chuppah
(ii) the ring
(iii) smashing the wine glass.
What do you think each of these adds to the significance of the ceremony?

*Task 3*
Study carefully the seven blessings which are part of the Jewish wedding ceremony and answer the following questions:

(a) What can you discover from them concerning what Jews believe about God?

(b) The sixth blessing is a reminder of the story in Genesis chapter 2 verses 18 to 25. Look this up in your Bible and say what is meant by the sentence in the blessing, 'thou didst gladden thy creature in the Garden of Eden.'

(c) It is said that in the seventh blessing six different words are used for 'joy' and four different words are used for 'love'. Write down the six words for 'joy' and the four for 'love'. Each of these words gives a slightly different insight into what it is hoped the marriage will be like. Briefly describe what you think each of them is saying.

(d) What do you think stands out most in these blessings to make them so appropriate for use at a marriage?

# 13

# Christian

John and Christine have been engaged to be married for about a year and, at last, the day of their wedding has come when, in an impressive and happy ceremony, they will begin their life as husband and wife.

## Preparations

We asked them sometime before the wedding about their plans.

*Our question:* Many people are married in a Registry Office, without a religious ceremony; why have you decided on a church wedding?

*Answer:* We want to be married in church because the church plays an important part in our lives. We go to worship regularly and it would be strange for us not to have a Christian ceremony to mark this special day. We believe it is important to ask God's blessing and help as we become man and wife.

*Our question:* Many people are married in a Christian church who seldom, if ever, go to worship; do you think they should be able to have a church wedding when, apparently, they are just 'using' the church?

*Answer:* Yes, we do. We feel that anyone who sincerely wants the blessing of God on their marriage should not be denied this.

*Our question:* We know you must have been very busy preparing for the wedding; there are so many matters which need your attention, such as sending out invitations, booking the reception, deciding what you will wear, and so on! Can you tell us what preparations there have been as far as the ceremony is concerned?

*Answer:* Yes. When we had decided on the date we went to see the Vicar of our church. He not only booked the date but also arranged for us to attend some classes which he holds with young couples like ourselves who are going to be married. In these classes we were made aware of the various parts of the marriage service and the practical details which would help everything go smoothly on the day. In addition we also discussed the meaning of the service and looked at ways in which our relationship could be strengthened: What if we have a quarrel? How can we understand each other's feelings? and many other important and helpful issues.

*Our question:* On the board outside the church it mentions 'the Solemnisation of Marriages'. Does that mean that the wedding in church will be a serious affair with everyone looking very solemn?

*Answer:* Not at all! In fact the Vicar mentioned that phrase to us and said that it meant 'an impressive religious ceremony' but at the same time he made it clear that he regarded the ceremony as one which has a strong note of joy and happiness running through it.

83

## The Ceremony

In the photograph you can see John and the 'Best Man', a friend who stands with the bridegroom in the service, sitting in the front pew waiting for Christine to arrive.

When she arrived, she walked down the aisle with her father, followed by her bridesmaids, to stand with John and the Best Man who had now left their seats and were standing facing the altar at the front of the church.

### Introduction

After the singing of a hymn, the Vicar read the following words from his book of services (of course where it says on the page '*N* and *N*', he said, 'John and Christine'):

> We have come together in the presence of God, to witness the marriage of *N* and *N*, to ask his blessing on them, and to share in their joy. Our Lord Jesus Christ was himself a guest at a wedding in Cana of Galilee, and through his Spirit he is with us now.
>
> The Scriptures teach us that marriage is a gift of God in creation and a means of his grace, a holy mystery in which man and woman become one flesh. It is God's purpose that, as husband and wife give themselves to each other in love throughout their lives, they shall be united in that love as Christ is united with his Church.
>
> Marriage is given, that husband and wife may comfort and help each other, living faithfully together in need and in plenty, in sorrow and in joy. It is given, that with delight and tenderness they may know each other in love, and, through the joy of their bodily union, may strengthen the union of their hearts and lives. It is given, that they may have children and be blessed in caring for them and bringing them up in accordance with God's will, to his praise and glory.

In marriage husband and wife belong to one another, and they begin a new life together in the community. It is a way of life that all should honour; and it must not be undertaken carelessly, lightly, or selfishly, but reverently, responsibly, and after serious thought.

This is the way of life, created and hallowed by God, that N and N are now to begin. They will each give their consent to the other; they will join hands and exchange solemn vows, and in token of this they will give and receive a ring.

Therefore, on this their wedding day we pray with them, that, strengthened and guided by God, they may fulfil his purpose for the whole of their earthly life together.

## Legal Requirements

The next two statements made by the Vicar are required by law, first he addressed the congregation:

'But first I am required to ask anyone present who knows a reason why these persons may not lawfully marry, to declare it now.'

No one raised any objections to the marriage of John and Christine, so he said to them:

'The vows you are about to take are to be made in the name of God, who is judge of all and who knows all the secrets of our hearts: therefore if either of you knows a reason why you may not lawfully marry, you must declare it now.'

The congregation were invited to stand for the next part of the ceremony. The Vicar addressed John:

'John, will you take Christine to be your wife? Will you love her, comfort her, honour and protect her, and, forsaking all others, be faithful to her as long as you both shall live?'

John answered: 'I will.'

Similar words were then put to Christine:

'Christine, will you take John to be your husband? Will you love him, comfort him, honour and protect him, and, forsaking all others, be faithful to him as long as you both shall live?'

Christine answered: 'I will.'

**The Vows**

The Vicar glanced in the direction of Christine's father and said, 'Who gives this woman to be married to this man?' Her father answered, 'I do.'

Some people think this sounds like an old-fashioned idea, as if the father owned his daughter, but was now prepared to give her to another man who would care for her! Others disagree and say that it is a part of the ceremony worth keeping for it is as if the father is saying, 'I care very deeply for my daughter, but I am happy for her to find joy in marriage.'

When Christine's father responded, the Vicar took her right hand and placed it in John's right hand; asking them to face each other, he told John to repeat after him the marriage vow:

'I, John, take you, Christine, to be my wife, to have and to hold from this day forward; for better, for worse, for richer, for poorer, in sickness and in health, to love and to cherish, till death us do part, according to God's holy law; and this is my solemn vow.'

Then it was Christine's turn:

'I, Christine, take you, John, to be my husband, to have and to hold from this day forward; for better, for worse, for richer, for poorer, in sickness and in health, to love and to cherish, till death us do part, according to God's holy law; and this is my solemn vow.'

## The Declaration

John and Christine were then declared to be husband and wife:

'In the presence of God, and before this congregation, John and Christine have given their consent and made their marriage vows to each other. They have declared their marriage by the joining of hands and by the giving and receiving of a ring. I therefore proclaim that they are husband and wife.'

The Vicar joined their right hands together and said:

'That which God has joined together, let not man divide.'

## The Ring

The Best Man passed the wedding ring to the Vicar who took it and offered the following blessing:

'Heavenly Father, by your blessing, let this ring be to John and Christine a symbol of unending love and faithfulness, to remind them of the vow and covenant which they have made this day, through Jesus Christ our Lord, Amen.'

He then passed the ring to John who placed it on the fourth finger of Christine's left hand and said:

'I give you this ring as a sign of our marriage. With my body I honour you, all that I am I give to you, and all that I have I share with you, within the love of God, Father, Son and Holy Spirit.'

Still holding hands, Christine replied:

'I receive this ring as a sign of our marriage. With my body I honour you, all that I am I give to you, and all that I have I share with you, within the love of God, Father, Son and Holy Spirit.'

## The Blessing

John and Christine knelt as the Vicar held up his hand over them in blessing and said:

86

'God the Father, God the Son, God the Holy Spirit, bless, preserve, and keep you; the Lord mercifully grant you the riches of his grace, that you may please him both in body and soul, and, living together in faith and love, may receive the blessings of eternal life. Amen.'

## Scripture Reading and Address

Everyone sat down after this and the Vicar read a passage from the Bible. He read the famous passage, chosen by Christine and John, from 1 Corinthians chapter 13 which is about love.

When he had finished this reading, he gave a very short talk in which he was speaking especially to John and Christine. He reminded them that, although this was a very joyous occasion, it was also a very serious one. The marriage service invites them to look at life realistically for it not only talks of joy but it also mentions sadness; it mentions birth *and* death, sickness *and* health, wealth *and* poverty. It could, he said, have only asked them to take marriage vows which talked of love, but instead, they were asked to take each other 'for better, for worse, for richer, for poorer, in sickness and in health . . . till death us do part'. He pointed out that by doing this, they are saying that they know love is stronger than all these and love can survive the problems which life may bring as well as enjoy the happiness it offers. With these and the other things he said, the Vicar gave John and Christine food for thought at the beginning of their life together.

## Conclusion

The last part of the service included another hymn, prayers and the final blessing:

'May God make you strong in faith and love, defend you on every side and guide you in truth and peace; and the blessing of God Almighty, the Father, the Son, and the Holy Spirit, be among you and remain with you always. Amen.'

John and Christine left the church, led by the Vicar and followed by the Best Man, bridesmaids and parents for the signing of the marriage register. This is a legal document which means that there is a permanent, signed record that John and Christine were married.

When this signing was completed, they re-entered the main body of the church and everyone stood as they walked down the aisle as man and wife. They came out of the church to the sound of the bells which were pealing to mark this happy occasion in their lives.

John and Christine are members of the Church of England so the order of service was one which is usually followed in that Church. If their marriage had been conducted by another Christian Church, for example if John and Christine were Methodists or Baptists or Roman Catholics, the ceremony might have been slightly different, but the essential parts would have been very similar. All Christian groups have a religious service to mark such an important event.

*Task 1*
Do you agree or disagree with what John and Christine said on page 83 about people being married in church? Give reasons for your answer.

*Task 2*
How important do you think preparation for marriage is? What do you think should be included in preparation classes such as those attended by John and Christine?

*Task 3*
(a) In the introduction to the Marriage Service three reasons are given for marriage. Write these reasons in your book in your own words.
(b) 'It must not be undertaken carelessly, lightly or selfishly but reverently, responsibly and after serious thought.'

In view of this sentence in the introductory part of the service, what would you advise a young couple to discuss seriously together about their future before they marry? What do you consider is meant by 'a responsible attitude to marriage'? Why should the word 'reverently' appear in a marriage service which takes place in church?

*Task 4*
Look again at the words of the Marriage Vows: express in your own words exactly what it is that John and Christine are promising. How difficult do you think it may be to keep such promises?

*Task 5*
In the service described in this section, the Bible reading was 1 Corinthians chapter 13: look this up in a Bible and list the qualities mentioned in verses 4 to 7 and say, for each, how you think they would strengthen a marriage.

# 14
# Muslim

The marriage of Ismail and Rahila had been arranged for some time before the ceremony took place.

Ismail had met Rahila when he was at college but he would not have dreamt of inviting her to go out with him or of ultimately asking her to marry him, since that would have been unacceptable to Muslim custom. He discussed his attraction to Rahila with his parents and his mother made enquiries about the girl and eventually approached Rahila's mother. The two mothers had many discussions so that each could find out sufficient information to decide whether Ismail and Rahila were suitable partners for each other.

Muslims defend this way of arranging a marriage by saying that after all it is married people who know what is important and what qualities make a good marriage.

The parents of Ismail and Rahila decided that these two were well-suited to each other, so Rahila was asked if she agreed to the marriage. Although the parents are so involved in the arrangement, the girl herself is quite free to make her own decision. Rahila had admired Ismail when she had met him and was happy to accept her mother's advice and agree to the marriage.

## The Dowry

Muslims think of marriage as a contract which is made before Allah, but practical arrangements for the future must enter into the discussions prior to the marriage. Among these is the fixing of a dowry; this is an agreed sum of money, depending on the circumstances of the families, which the bridegroom will pay to his bride. It is often paid in two parts: some is paid before the marriage to help the bride and her family prepare for the wedding. The other part is usually only paid if at any time in the future the marriage breaks down. In this way the woman is given some measure of security if the marriage should end. Sometimes the first part of the dowry is paid partly in goods which will be useful in the couple's home; this was the case in the marriage of Ismail and Rahila and in the photograph you can see Rahila's mother examining some of the items from the trunk which has been sent by Ismail and his family.

89

The dowry is referred to by the word **Mahr** and the Qur'an lays down that it is the wife's property and must not be taken away from her. It is regarded as a sign that the husband respects his bride as a person in her own right.

## The Marriage Ceremony

### At the Bridegroom's Home

On the day of the marriage, some of the close family guests assembled at Ismail's home. Prayers were said by Ismail's father as they waited for the guests to arrive; on the table lay a plate of sweetmeats so that hospitality could be offered to the guests to make them welcome. Once they had all arrived, more prayers were said. You can see Ismail, dressed in a long white garment, sharing in these prayers before the rest of the wedding garments are put on.

Ismail's grandfather helped to put on the bridegroom's white head covering which was followed by a very decorative head-dress, according to the customs of Muslims from Pakistan, the homeland of Ismail's family. This had no particular religious significance but was a reminder of a time when the bridegroom and bride would not have seen each other until the ceremony had been performed. When all this was done, guests gave gifts to Ismail, most of which were gifts of money which were pinned to his clothes; you can see that many of the gifts were very generous!

When everyone was ready, Ismail and his family and guests made their way to Rahila's home where the ceremony was to take place.

### At the Bride's Home

We arrived at Rahila's home and were welcomed by her father; we were shown into a room prepared for the ceremony, but there was no sign of the bride. We were told that customs vary among Muslims and sometimes the bridegroom and the bride take marriage vows in each other's hearing, but at other times the witnesses hear the vows and pass word to the other partner that the promises have been made. At this wedding, it was the latter custom which was followed.

We heard Ismail make a declaration which was something like the following:

'I, Ismail, take Rahila as my lawfully married wife before Allah and in the presence of these witnesses, in accordance with the teaching of the Holy Qur'an. I promise to do everything to make this marriage an act of obedience to Allah, to make it a relationship of love, mercy, peace and faithfulness. Let Allah be my witness, for he is the best of all witnesses.'

The bridegroom wearing his head-dress (right)

Two of those present went to the other room where Rahila was waiting and assured her and the witnesses present there that the marriage vow had been made. They heard Rahila agree, in similar words, to the marriage and they returned with word of this to Ismail.

The Imam was present and he produced a certificate which he signed and which was signed by Ismail. Once this was done, and the witnesses also signed, it was taken for Rahila's signature.

The Imam led Ismail and the other men present in prayers for the marriage. When the prayers were ended, one of Ismail's friends stepped forward and put a ring on the bridegroom's finger.

After this had been done, the door opened to show some of the women standing outside; one of the young women, a friend of Rahila, entered carrying a tray on which was a plate of traditional Asian sweetmeats, and a glass of milk.

The bridegroom's ring

This was offered to Ismail and he ate a few of the sweetmeats and drank some of the milk. It was explained to us that this was an old custom and the offering of

The certificate

food and drink was supposed to help ensure that the bridegroom would soon father children. We were also told that often the women play a joke on the bridegroom by putting chilli powder or salt into the milk, but the bridegroom still has to drink it!

Soon after this, we all left for a hall in which the wedding reception had been prepared; again, however, men and women had the wedding meal in different rooms. It was, nevertheless, a very happy occasion and all the guests seemed to enjoy themselves immensely.

# Muslim Views on Marriage

Naturally, witnessing such a marriage raised certain questions in our minds since the ceremony was so different to those we are used to in the West. As soon as we had the opportunity, we put our questions to some of those present.

*Our question:* Since the bride was not even in the same room as the bridegroom for the ceremony, it appears to us that the woman is of considerably less importance than the man! Is this really the Muslim view?

*Answer:* Not at all! Certainly it is true that Muslims believe that the husband is the one responsible for running the affairs of the family, but this does not mean that the woman is unimportant. We are very careful to protect her rights. You have already seen that when the marriage is arranged, a dowry is agreed and that it becomes the wife's property. Muslim husbands are urged to honour and respect their wives; this is emphasised very much in the teaching of the Holy Qur'an. There is a saying in Muslim tradition: 'The best among you are those who are kindest to their wives.'

*Our question:* We hope that Ismail and Rahila will be very happy, but suppose that they are not: is divorce permitted among Muslims?

*Answer:* Yes it is, but it does not occur very often. It is reported that Muhammad the Prophet said, 'Of all things permitted by law, divorce is the most hateful in the sight of Allah.' Nevertheless, Muslims are realistic enough to see that if a husband and wife find it impossible to live together in happiness, it is better for them to part. The Qur'an says, 'If you fear a split between a man and his wife, send for an arbiter (i.e someone who will help sort out the problem) from his family and an arbiter from her family. If both want to be reconciled, Allah will bring them together again.' Many Muslim families would follow this advice and try to help the couple sort out their problem. If this fails, then they could be divorced and would be free to enter into another marriage if they wished.

*Our question:* Do you think the fact that the marriage has been arranged by the parents has anything to do with there being fewer divorces among Muslims?

*Answer:* Yes, we do! Parents care very deeply about their children and want what is best for them. They take great care to ensure that the marriage partner is one with whom there is the best chance of happiness.

*Our question:* We understand that Muslims are allowed more than one wife: is this so and how widely is this practised?

*Answer:* The Qur'an says: 'You may marry such women as may seem good to you, two, three or four. But if you fear that you cannot maintain equality among them, then marry one only.' There have been and still are occasions when Muslims have had more than one wife, but not, of course, in Britain; we must abide by the law of the land in which we are living. Many Muslims would, in fact, say that when Muhammad gave this advice, he was really saying that we should only have one wife, for it is virtually impossible to treat several wives with equality!

*Our question:* Ismail and Rahila are both Muslims; would Muslim parents ever agree to their son or daughter marrying a non-Muslim?

*Answer:* We would prefer our sons to marry Muslim girls and most Muslim parents would not approve of the marriage of a daughter to a non-Muslim man. We would, however, discuss this with the family very carefully and we would never use force to prevent a marriage for that is against the teaching of Islam.

We came away from the wedding feeling that although the marriage of Ismail and Rahila had been different from most marriages in the West, nevertheless, Muslims had very definite well-thought out views on marriage, based on their strong religious beliefs. The final good wishes of the guests were expressed in words which meant, 'May Allah bless you and may his benediction be upon you', as Ismail and Rahila began their life together.

## Task 1
Married people know the qualities needed for a good marriage.'

(a) Write a conversation between a Muslim boy or girl and a parent where the child is questioning the Muslim tradition of the arranged marriage.

(b) What qualities do you think are important for a good marriage? How far do you think these would be different from those that parents might look for?

## Task 2
(a) Explain the purpose of the dowry in a Muslim marriage.

(b) If the dowry is partly in goods rather than money, what items would you consider might be included?

(c) What words and actions during the marriage ceremony show clearly that it was a religious ceremony and not just the making of a legal contract?

## Task 3
Prayers played a considerable part in the Muslim marriage ceremony; what personal prayers might have been offered at this time by (a) the bride or bridegroom and (b) the parents of those being married?

## Task 4
The giving of food and drink to the bridegroom was a reminder that one purpose of marriage is to have children. Muslims regard the family as very important; how important do *you* think children might be to a marriage? Give reasons for your answer.

## Task 5
Although Muslims permit divorce, they remember the saying, 'Of all things permitted by law, divorce is the most hateful in the sight of Allah.' What reasons might be given for saying that God dislikes divorce so much?

# 15
# Sikh

Most Sikhs, like the majority of Hindus and Muslims, practise arranged marriages, i.e. the parents find one whom they consider to be a suitable partner for their son or daughter to marry.

One very important fact about a Sikh marriage is that it must take place in the presence of the holy book, the Guru Granth Sahib. This is regarded as the chief witness to the marriage and forms a focal point for the whole ceremony.

After marriage a Sikh girl will go to live in her husband's family home, so marriage in Sikhism is really an affair involving two families and not simply the couple. It is, therefore, important that the bride chosen should be a Sikh girl who will not only be suitable as a partner for her husband but will also fit in well with his family.

The marriage need not take place at the gurdwara, i.e. the temple, although it often does; it could be conducted at the bride's home, or at any other place to which the Granth has been taken in a proper manner. The Granth must be treated with great reverence and held above the head when it is being carried to the place where the ceremony is to occur. Once there, it should be placed on a raised platform and covered by a **Romalla,** an embroidered cover. Above the Granth a canopy should be erected, as a sign of honour and respect for its authority as a living guru or teacher.

## The Ceremony

Jasbinder Kaur Bains was not married in the gurdwara; her family hired the use of a large hall and arranged for the Granth to be placed there. Jasbinder was married in the morning, as is the case with most Sikh weddings. At 10 a.m. the family and friends of Jasbinder and her future husband, Saminder, began to arrive at the hall. The invitation read: '10 a.m.: tea and milni'. Milni is the word used for the meeting together of the two sets of families and friends. At eleven o'clock, everyone was seated on the carpeted floor and the hall resembled a gurdwara: men sat on the right-hand side, and women on the left; all were facing the Guru Granth Sahib.

The service began with the musicians singing the Sikh morning hymn; during this Saminder came forward to take his place in front of the holy book.

Jasbinder was led into the hall by a friend who was to attend her and help her throughout the ceremony. When she had taken her place on the left-hand side of Saminder, a prayer was said asking for God's blessing on the couple.

The hymn which followed illustrates the Sikh attitude to any important event in life. The musicians sang:

'Before undertaking anything,
Seek the grace of God.
By the grace of the true Guru,
Who in the company of the saints
Expounds the truth,
Success is attained.
It is with the true Guru
That we taste heavenly bliss.'

Prior to the actual ceremony, the person
who was conducting the service explained
the significance of Sikh marriage. He
said that the purpose of marriage was to
unite two souls so that spiritually they
become one. In order to achieve this
union, Saminder must love, respect and
support his wife; Jasbinder, for her part,
must return his love and be loyal to him
both in times of good and bad fortune.
The couple were told to work towards
unity physically, materially,
intellectually, emotionally and spiritually.

They were given the advice of Guru Amar Das, one of the Ten Gurus of the Sikh faith:

The bride should know no other man except her husband, so the Guru ordains. She alone is of good family, she alone shines with light who is adorned with the love of her husband. There is only one way to the heart of the beloved: to be humble and true and do his bidding; only thus is true union attained. They are not man and wife who only have physical contact; only they are wedded truly who have one spirit in two bodies.

Ask the happy one by what ways they have won the beloved. They answer: By sweetness of speech and the beauty of contentment. A loaf of dry bread and bare earth for a bed, in the company of the beloved is full of happiness. Let humility be the word, resignation be the offering, the tongue be the mint of sweet speech. Adopt these habits, dear sister, then you will have him in your power.

Another person's property, another man's wife, talking ill of another, poisons one's life. Like the touch of a poisonous snake is the touch of another man's wife.

After the duties involved in marriage had been outlined, the couple were asked whether they wished to be married. They showed their willingness for the service to proceed by bowing before the Granth.

Mr Bains came forward and put one end of the scarf which Saminder was wearing into his right hand; he placed the other end into his daughter's hand. As the couple were symbolically joined together in this way, the musicians sang:

'Praise and blame I both forsake,
I seize the edge of your garment,
All else I let pass.
All relationships I have found false;
I cling to thee, my Lord.'

The couple symbolically joined

uru Granth Sahib opened

## The Lavan

When this hymn was finished, the Guru Granth Sahib was opened at the **Lavan**, a hymn composed by Guru Ram Das, another of the Ten Gurus, for his own daughter's wedding. After the first verse was read, Saminder and Jasbinder slowly walked round the Granth both still holding the scarf which joined them; and as they walked that same verse was sung:

In the first round, the Lord ordains for you a secular life.
Accept the Guru's word as your scripture and it will free you from sin.
Let your law of life be to meditate on the Name of God
Which is the theme of all scriptures.
Contemplate the true Guru, the perfect Guru

And all your sins shall depart.
Fortunate are those who hold God in their hearts;
They are ever serene and happy.
God's servant declares that in the first round,
The marriage rite has begun.'

They sat down in their positions at the front to listen to the words of the second verse of the Lavan:

'In the second round, the Lord has caused you to meet the true Guru.
The fear in your hearts has departed And the filth of egoism has been washed away.
Imbued with the fear of God and by singing his praises,
You behold his very presence.

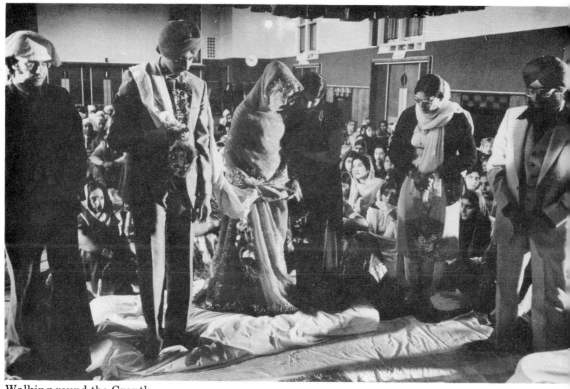

Walking round the Granth

The Lord God is the Soul of the Universe.
And his presence pervades every place,
Within and without is the One God
And in the company of the saints the songs of joy are sung.
God's servant proclaims that in the second round,
The divine strains of ecstasy are heard.'

For the second time, they walked around the Granth. This procedure was repeated after each of the other two verses of the Lavan:

'In the third round, love for the Lord stirs in the heart
And the mind becomes detached from worldly things.
'Through the company of the saints and by the great good fortune,
I have met the Lord.

I have found the Immaculate Lord by singing his praises
And uttering his hymns.
Good fortune has brought me into the company of saints
Where tales of the Ineffable are told.
My heart is now absorbed in the Name of God
In accordance with the destiny written for me.
Nanak declares that in the third round,
Divine love and detachment are born in the heart.'

'In the fourth round, divine knowledge awakes in the mind
And union with God is complete.
Through the Guru's instruction the union is made easy.
And the sweetness of the Beloved pervades my body and soul.
Dear and pleasing is the Lord to me

nd I remain ever absorbed in him.
y singing the Lord's praises
have attained my heart's desire.
od has completed this marriage
nd the bride's heart rejoices in his
ame.
anak proclaims that in the fourth
und
ou have obtained God as the Everlasting
ridegroom.'

n this fourth walk round the Granth,
ie congregation showered them with
ose petals as a sign of congratulation,
r now they were man and wife.
The words of the Lavan, the Sikh
arriage hymn, tell us a great deal
oout Sikh religious thought. These
ords give the couple good advice which
uru Ram Das, no doubt, hoped his
aughter would heed. They also show
ow love can grow as the marriage
atures, but more importantly they
lustrate how Sikhs believe union with
od may be achieved. Just as at marriage
vo people enter into a relationship
ith each other, so man can choose to
nter into a relationship with God. As a
ood marriage develops, two souls become

one; the couple are completely united
spiritually, while remaining two distinct
individuals; as an inner knowledge of
God grows, a man becomes aware of a
deeper union with his Creator.
The Lavan gives some clues as to how
best to grow in knowledge of God. This
knowledge is to be obtained by living a
normal family life, meditating on God's
Name and following the teaching of the
Gurus. It is particularly in what Sikhs
call the **Sangat**, i.e. the fellowship of the
Sikh congregation, that knowledge of
God can grow and selfishness and
attachment to worldly things disappear.
So a person may become full of divine
knowledge and find perfect joy.

## Conclusion
The Granthi, who had been reading the
words of the Lavan, left his place behind
the holy book to join the congregation.
Everyone stood for the Ardas, the last
prayer said in a Sikh act of worship.
The final part of the ceremony was
when the Granth was opened at random
and a passage from the book was read
before everyone received a portion of
Karah Parshad.

he Ardas

The ceremony itself being over, the wedding celebrations began with the parents of the couple coming forward to bless them and to place garlands around their necks. The celebrations continued until four o'clock in the afternoon when Jasbinder left to go to Saminder's home to become a part of his family.

### Task 1
Write out the words of the Lavan which show how to achieve a perfect relationship with God. Can you think of reasons why such advice about a relationship with God is being given at a marriage?

### Task 2
Jasbinder's friend assisted her a great deal both before and during the ceremony; imagine you are this friend and write a description of your duties.
*or*
Imagine that you are Mr Bains, Jasbinder's father, and describe the arrangements you made before the wedding and the part you played in the ceremony.

### Task 3
Explain how and why the Granth is regarded as the most important witness to the marriage.

### Task 4
(a) 'A loaf of dry bread and bare earth for a bed, in the company of the beloved, is full of happiness.' What do you think is meant by this?

(b) 'Let humility be the word,
Resignation be the offering,
The tongue the mint of sweet speech.
Adopt these habits, dear sister,
Then you will have him in your power.'
What do you think of this advice which is being given to the bride?

## Additional Tasks on Marriage Ceremonies

1 (a) How important is a religious marriage ceremony in your opinion? What do you think the religious ceremony adds to the occasion, which may help the future life of the couple?

(b) Write a paragraph beginning
*either*
I would wish to be married at a religious ceremony because. . .
*or*
I would wish to be married at a civil ceremony in the Registry Office because. . .

2 Should a man and woman who follow different religions marry? What problems do you think they might have to face in such a marriage?

3 What arguments can you present either in favour of, or against, your future husband or wife being chosen by your parents?

4 Love and marriage is the theme of the vast majority of pop songs in many parts of the world; why do you think this is so? What ideas about love and marriage do many of these songs convey? Illustrate your answer by referring to some of the songs you know.

# Part IV

# Death

# 16

# Hindu

When a Hindu living in Britain dies, the relatives have to make certain adjustments to the traditional funeral ceremonies which would be carried out if the death had occurred in India, their country of origin. For example, in India, the cremation of the body would take place just outside the village on an open funeral pyre, but in Britain this is not permitted so they have to make use of the services of the local crematorium.

## The Funeral

When Mr Sharma died, his family carried out as many of the traditional rituals as they could. The eldest son washed the body and dressed it in new clothes, rubbed the sweet-smelling sandalwood paste on to his father's forehead and whispered the word for God into his ear. By carrying out such rituals, Mr Sharma's son was preparing his father's soul for entry into a new sphere of activity, for Hindus believe that the soul, which they call the **Atman**, never dies.

A service took place at the local crematorium; a Hindu priest was invited to conduct the prayers and to chant appropriate words from the Hindu holy books. Among the passages read were:

'May your eyesight return to the sun,
Your breath to the winds,
May your waters mingle with the ocean
And your earthly parts become one with the earth.'

Since in India the eldest son would have had the task of lighting the funeral pyre, Mr Sharma's son pressed the button in the crematorium which was the signal for the curtains to draw, hiding the coffin from view. He and his brothers were also permitted to go and see the coffin being placed in the cremator.

After the service at the crematorium, the family returned home and observed a twelve-day period of mourning during which prayers were especially offered for the departed soul of Mr Sharma.

Mrs Sharma was now wearing a white sari because white is the traditional symbol of mourning among Hindus. It was noticeable that she had also removed most of her jewellery as a sign of her widowhood.

## Death in India

Mr Sharma's son, Surbjit, talked to us about the funeral and the Hindu view of death. He said he remembered his grandfather's death in India and how the family had been totally responsible for the cremation. He produced photographs of the occasion; the one on this page shows grandfather Sharma prior to his cremation.

Surjit told us that his father made the traditional preparations just as he had done. Cremation, in India, was carried out as soon as possible after death because of the hot climate. There was no coffin such as was provided for his father; the body was simply taken on a stretcher to the cremation ground, a piece of land outside the village, covered only by a piece of cloth. Here a **kunda** had been prepared; this is a trench dug out of the ground about a metre wide and two metres deep. The sides were lined with wood or bricks and it was filled with pieces of wood on which the dead body was laid.

Surjit said that practically everyone in the village followed the funeral procession to the kunda. The body was laid on the wood in the kunda and covered by more wood, then his father, as the eldest son, lit the funeral pyre by first lighting the wood at the head and then at the feet.

A Hindu priest had been present at this cremation and he recited verses from the Vedas, the holy books, as the body burned. Surjit's father had kept the fire burning by making offerings of ghee which he poured on to the fire with a large ladle.

The mourners stayed at the cremation ground until the fire had burned down, then three days later they returned to collect the ashes which were later scattered on the River Ganges. 'My father's ashes also', he said, 'have been collected from the crematorium, and we have sent them to relatives in India so that they can scatter them on the water of the Ganges.

We asked Surjit to tell us why most Hindus wish their ashes to be taken to the Ganges. He replied, 'It is the dearest wish of a Hindu who is nearing the end of his life, to be near Mata Ganges, that is, Mother Ganges, for to Hindus it is a sacred river. Many who are ill make their way to Benares, a city on the banks of the Ganges, so that when they die their bodies may be burned on the steps leading down to the river, which are known as **ghats.** In this way, they feel sure that their ashes will be scattered on the river and carried away by its waters. It is believed that to die in such a holy place means that there is a better chance of never being reborn again.'

104

The body is cremated

# Hindu Belief about Death

We asked Surbjit to explain what he meant when he talked of 'a better chance of never being reborn again'. We learned that, at its simplest, Hindu belief is that a man's soul will never die, but will be born in a new form to live again and be given another opportunity to obtain release from the cycle of rebirth, so that he can be at one with God. The rebirth is known as **Reincarnation** or **Samsara** and the release is called by Hindus, **Moksha**. According to Hindu belief, therefore, we have lived on earth many times, but, of course, do not remember these previous existences because we must live again with no previous knowledge of life except what we have accumulated in spiritual knowledge. The Hindu says that man must strive to build up his spiritual knowledge and eventually cast aside the distractions of the world.

Surbjit said, 'We Hindus talk about **Maya**, which means 'illusion'; what we mean is that on earth we become involved with being successful, having a lot of money and possessions, and such things make us forget about the true purpose of life. When death comes, all this has to be given up, for we can take nothing with us when we die, so it has all proved to be an illusion – Maya. If a person has based his whole life on Maya, then he will be born again until the truth is learned about the real purpose of life.'

We asked how Hindus consider this truth is to be learned. How can someone obtain Moksha – release from the continual round of death and rebirth? The answer we were given was that there are three ways in which the Hindu believes this can be achieved:

(1) A person can achieve Moksha by building up a good **Karma**. Reference has been made to this elsewhere and you will remember that Karma means 'action which results in a reaction'; in other words, you cannot expect anything you do, not to create some result. For example, if you are unpleasant to someone you will probably find that person is unpleasant to you. The Hindu believes that many actions do not create an immediate effect, but the results will be seen eventually, if not in this life, then in the next. If a person has been evil, he cannot expect rebirth as a human being; he may first have to go through a series of rebirths as an animal or even an insect. If a man wishes to build up a good Karma he must live his life wisely and treat other people with respect.

(2) A second way of helping to achieve Moksha is by studying the scriptures in order to obtain knowledge of God.

(3) A third way, which is clearly linked to the second, is to show devotion to God in prayer and service.

By making efforts in all three of these ways, the Hindu hopes to be released from rebirth and to obtain that for which his soul longs – oneness with Aum – God.

In the Hindu scriptures it says:

'This soul within my heart is smaller than a grain of rice or barley or mustard or millet, or a kernel of millet.
This soul within my heart is greater than the earth, the air, the sky
And all the worlds.
This is my soul within my heart.
This is the All.
And when I die, I shall merge into it.'

'When his clothes wear out, a man puts them away and takes new and different ones; and so the embodied soul will put away the worn out bodies and take new and other ones.'

The warning is also given:

'According to one's deeds so does one become; the doer of good becomes good; the doer of evil becomes evil.'

Holding such beliefs, Surbjit assured us that death is not something to be feared. 'Of course,' he said, 'death brings sadness. I will miss my father very much indeed; but he was a good man and his goodness will have its reward.'

*Task 1*
Write a description of a Hindu cremation in India; try to include in your account something about the beliefs of those who practise such a ceremony, and what you think you would feel as you watched the ceremony.

*Task 2*
What does the term **Maya** mean? What do you think a Hindu would consider to be Maya and why would he think this was so? What do you consider to be Maya in your life? Give reasons for your answer.

*Task 3*
In what practical ways might someone try to build up a good **Karma**? Describe the other ways in which a Hindu believes he can obtain **Moksha.**

*Task 4*
Write an argument (a) in favour of, and (b) against, the belief in reincarnation.

106

# 17
# Jewish

Regardless of which religion you follow, it is difficult, if not impossible, not to feel sad when someone whom you love dies. Jews recognise this and their customs and practices following a death are such that they not only allow but actually help grief to be expressed.

The Steinberg family were kind enough to discuss with us how they faced up to a death in their family and gave us an insight into their traditions and customs.

## Facing up to Death

Abraham Steinberg had been ill for some time and he knew that he was dying. He reached a point where he obviously felt that the end was near because he called his wife and sons around him and asked for his prayer book. The Jewish prayer book has a page headed, 'Confession on a Death Bed' and it was at that page that he wanted the book opened. As best as he could, Mr Steinberg read the words of the prayer which expressed the idea that if God wants his life to end, he is ready to accept it. The prayer also asked God to protect his family and it ended with the words, 'Into thy hand I commend my spirit . . . O Lord God of truth. Amen.'

Since he could not manage to read the rest of the page, his son read the Hebrew words for him. You can see both the Hebrew and the English on this page.

When Mr Steinberg died, the members of his family did something which non-

בשעת יציאת הנשמה:

יְיָ מֶלֶךְ· יְיָ מָלָךְ· יְיָ ׀ יִמְלוֹךְ לְעוֹלָם וָעֶד:

*(To be said three times.)*

בָּרוּךְ שֵׁם כְּבוֹד מַלְכוּתוֹ לְעוֹלָם וָעֶד:

*(To be said three times.)*

יְיָ הוּא הָאֱלֹהִים:

*(To be said seven times.)*

שְׁמַע יִשְׂרָאֵל יְיָ אֱלֹהֵינוּ יְיָ אֶחָד:

*When the end is approaching :—*

The Lord reigneth; the Lord hath reigned; the Lord shall reign for ever and ever.    *(To be said three times.)*

Blessed be his name, whose glorious kingdom is for ever and ever.    *(To be said three times.)*

The Lord he is God.    *(To be said seven times.)*

Hear, O Israel: the Lord our God, the Lord is one.

Jewish observers would have considered strange: each one took hold of the garment he or she was wearing and tore it! This is a very old Jewish tradition which is often mentioned in the scriptures. Many Jews today say that such an action has value for it is a way of expressing anger and shock that, quite naturally, they feel on the death of a loved one; they are venting the anger they feel on the garment and in so doing are getting rid of some of the emotion which has built up.

A candle was lit and this was placed near Mr Steinberg's head. One of his sons remained with the body and quietly recited some of the Psalms. From now until the burial, the body would not be left alone.

Arrangements were made straight away for the funeral, for it is the tradition among Jews to bury the body, if at all possible, within about twenty-four hours of the death. The undertaker provided a very plain, simple wooden coffin and, before the body of Mr Steinberg was placed in it, his tallith, i.e. his prayer shawl, was wrapped around him. A tallith has fringes at each end and these had been removed. This is because the fringes symbolise the 613 religious rules which Jews believe they are to observe; now that Abraham Steinberg is dead, he no longer has to fulfil such earthly requirements.

A Jewish cemetery

# The Funeral

### At the Home
Mr Steinberg's funeral took place on the day after his death. Before leaving for the cemetery, the Rabbi from the synagogue which the Steinbergs attend, conducted a brief service in the home. He read some passages from the scriptures which included words appropriate to the occasion such as:

'So teach us to number our days, that we may get a heart of wisdom.'

'As for man, his days are as grass; as the flower of the field, so he flourishes. For the wind passes over it and it is gone; and the place thereof shall know it no more. But the loving kindness of the Lord is from everlasting to everlasting upon them that fear him.'

The Rabbi also said a prayer:

'O Lord, who art full of compassion, grant pardon of sins and perfect rest beneath the shadow of thy divine presence in the exalted places among the holy and pure, who shine as the brightness of the firmament, to Abraham Steinberg who has gone to his eternal home.

O Lord of compassion, remember him for all the good and pious deeds he did while on earth. Open to him the gates of righteousness and light. Shelter him for evermore, under the cover of thy wings. Amen.'

## At the Prayer Hall

One of the local cemeteries has a corner which is specially reserved for the Jewish community. It was rather noticeable that whereas in the rest of the cemetery the gravestones varied considerably in size and style, here all the stones were of roughly the same size and shape. Jews believe that in death all are equal and there should be no difference between the funerals of rich and poor.

The funeral party travelled from the Steinbergs' home to the cemetery where other friends were waiting. The mourners followed the coffin into a small building known as a Prayer Hall where another short service took place.

Many of the words read by the Rabbi emphasised the idea that Abraham Steinberg's death should be accepted as the will of God:

'The Rock, perfect in every work; who can say unto him, What workest thou? He ruleth below and above; he causes death and he revives . . . The Lord gave and the Lord has taken away; blessed be the name of the Lord.'

A Psalm also was read which gave words of comfort to the mourners. In addition a tribute to Mr Steinberg was given by someone who had known him well.

## At the Graveside

When the mourners left the Prayer Hall for the graveside, members of the family and close friends carried the coffin. As it was lowered into the grave, the Rabbi said, 'May he come to his place in peace.' Everyone present then shovelled some earth into the grave to fill it up. Many Jews say that though it may seem unfeeling to expect family and friends to do this, it actually helps them to accept the fact of their loved one's death. As the close family mourners left the graveside the others present said, 'May the Lord comfort you among the other mourners of Zion and Jerusalem.'

As they all made their way back to the Prayer Hall, they each plucked a few blades of grass and said:

'And they of the city shall flourish like the grass of the earth.'

This is a way of saying that although Abraham Steinberg is dead, life goes on.

## The Kaddish

A final, brief service took place in the Prayer Hall, but before entering, the mourners washed their hands; this is why you can see a towel hanging on the door of the Prayer Hall in the photograph on p.110. As they washed, they said:

'He makes death to vanish in life eternal; and the Lord God wipes away tears off all faces.'

The main part of this brief service was a prayer known as the **Kaddish**, i.e. a prayer which glorifies God's name. This particular Kaddish was recited by Mr Steinberg's sons, following the usual custom. At the end of the prayer, all present made the response:

The Prayer Hall

they express their grief, which aids recovery from the shock of the death and enables them to come to terms with it.

Morning and evening prayers are said in the home. The prayers in the Steinbergs' home included passages like:

'O Lord and King, in whose hands are the souls of the living and the dead, receive, in thy great loving kindness, the soul of Abraham Steinberg . . . Shelter his soul in the shadow of thy wings: make known to him the path of life.'

Always the prayers ended with the Kaddish, the prayer which glorifies God's name, being recited by the sons. This daily reciting of the Kaddish will continue for eleven months. The recitation of such a prayer which praises and glorifies God, keeps reminding the family of their faith and its importance for all of life.

'Let his great name be blessed for ever and to all eternity.'

## After the Funeral

The Steinberg family returned home and ate a meal after the funeral; this is often called 'the meal of comfort' and it consisted of hard-boiled eggs and bread. Not much comfort in that, you might say! Jews say that the egg is a symbol of life in the midst of death, and that its roundness represents the continuous nature of life. Bread is described as 'the staff of life'.

The period starting with the day of the funeral is known as **Shiva** and lasts for seven days. During this time it is the custom for relatives and friends to call at the home. The mourners sit on low stools and are encouraged to talk about their loved one who has died, and in this way

## Unveiling the Tombstone

A year after Mr Steinberg's death, another ceremony will take place at the cemetery, like the one you can see in the photograph.

## The Anniversary of Death – Yahrzeit

Each year on the anniversary of the death, Mr Steinberg will be especially remembered. The Jew talks of **Yahrzeit,** i.e. the anniversary. Some of the family recite the Kaddish and in the home a candle is lit on the eve of Yahrzeit and it burns for twenty-four hours. In many synagogues there are small memorial plaques with the name of the deceased and each one has a little light which is turned on for the anniversary of the death. Many say that the light is a reminder that a man's soul is like a light kindled by God.

A headstone will be erected at the grave and when family and friends come for the ceremony, they will see it covered with a cloth. Psalms will be recited and prayers said, including the Kaddish. Finally, the cloth will be removed and the inscription read aloud. So the memory of Abraham Steinberg will be kept alive. As mourners leave the grave they wash their hands, as they did at the time of the funeral; you can also see in the photograph on page 110 two collecting boxes; this is so that gifts of money may be made to a Jewish organisation in memory of the dead person.

## Jewish Belief about Death

If we study the earlier parts of Jewish scripture, we find that Jews at one time had no belief in a real life after death. They tended to believe that God rewarded goodness with a long life and a large family! He punished wrong doing by sending suffering. As time went on, however, it became clear that this was not really true; good people sometimes died young; evil people sometimes did not seem to suffer much. So they gradually came to believe in another life where God would reward the good and judge the evil and this is how most Jews think about it now. This belief is expressed in words from the Jewish Book of Daily Prayer, which many Jews use for their own private meditation:

'This world is like a vestibule before the world to come; prepare yourself in the vestibule that you may enter into the hall.'

Some Jews believe that at Creation, God made everyone's soul. When a person dies, the soul goes to **Olam Ha'ba**, i.e. a world to come. (Some believe that it takes one year for the soul to get to Olam Ha'ba; others say that it is only the souls of the wicked that take so long and that they go to a place of suffering for at least a year. This, they say, is why the regular recitation of the Kaddish by the sons of the dead person only goes on for eleven months; if they continued for a year it might imply that they regarded the dead person as wicked!)

Another belief held by many Jews is that all souls remain at rest until all the souls made by God have been 'used up'; it is then that **Yom Din**, i.e. the Day of Judgement, will come, when the righteous will enjoy a closer relationship with God.

It is interesting to note that Jews refer to a cemetery as **Bet Hayyim** which means 'House of Life'. This is another of the ways in which they express their strong belief that death is not the end.

*Task 1*
Choose four of the rituals observed by Jews during the period from death to the first anniversary. In what ways does each of the rituals you have chosen help the mourners?

*Task 2*
How do Jews honour the memory of someone who has died? What other ways can you think of to honour the memory of a loved one?

*Task 3*
Explain what you think is meant by the words, 'This world is like a vestibule before the world to come; prepare yourself in the vestibule that you may enter into the hall.' What preparation do you think is intended?

*Task 4*
The following story is told of a Jewish Rabbi who lived in the Second Century CE:

'Rabbi Meir had two young sons whom he and his wife loved very dearly. Both sons died on the same day; it was the Sabbath and he was in the House of Learning, teaching his people about their faith.

On his return, his wife greeted him with a question: "Some time ago a friend gave me some jewels to keep for him. Today, he demands their return; what shall I do?" The Rabbi replied, "I cannot understand you asking such a question; you must, of course, return the jewels." His wife took him by the hand and led him to the room where their two children lay dead. "These", she said, "are the jewels I must return." The Rabbi, through his tears, spoke words from the scriptures "The Lord gave and the Lord has taken away; blessed be the name of the Lord."

Write a few sentences saying what you think about the attitude of the Rabbi and his wife to the death of their children.

# 18
# Christian

As the coffin emerged from the church, this marked the end of the first part of the funeral for Mary White. This was the church she had attended for many years and it was fitting that the family should follow the custom observed in most Christian churches and bring her body here for a funeral service.

## The Service in Church

At the beginning of the short service, the Minister read some words from the Bible as the coffin was brought in and placed at the front of the church. Mrs White's husband and family followed and sat in the front pews. The verses which were used in this part of the service were:

'Jesus said, I am the resurrection, and I am the life; he who believes in me, though he die, yet shall he live, and whoever lives and believes in me shall never die.' (John 11 verses 25 to 26)
'We brought nothing into the world, and we take nothing out. The Lord gives, and the Lord takes away: blessed be the name of the Lord.' (1 Timothy 6 verse 7 and Job 1 (verse 21)
'The eternal God is your refuge, and underneath are the everlasting arms.' (Deuteronomy 33 verse 27)
'The steadfast love of the Lord never ceases, his compassion never fails: every morning they are renewed.' (Lamentations 3 verses 22 to 23)
'Blessed are those who mourn, for they shall be comforted.' (Matthew 5 verse 4)
'I am sure that neither death, nor life, nor angels, nor principalities, nor powers, nor things present, nor things to come, nor height, nor depth, nor anything else in all creation, will be able to separate us from the love of God in Christ Jesus our Lord.' (Romans 8 verses 38 to 39)

Following this, we all said together:

'Heavenly Father, in your Son Jesus Christ you have given us a true faith and a sure hope. Strengthen this faith and hope in us all our days, that we may live as those who believe in the communion of saints, the forgiveness of sins, and the resurrection to eternal life; through your Son Jesus Christ our Lord. Amen.'

We then sang a hymn which is often used at funerals; it is based on the words of Psalm 23:

The Lord's my Shepherd, I'll not want.
    He makes me down to lie
In pastures green: he leadeth me
    The quiet waters by.
My soul he doth restore again;
    And me to walk doth make
Within the paths of righteousness,
    Even for his own Name's sake.
Yea, though I walk in death's dark vale,
    Yet will I fear none ill:
For thou art with me; and thy rod
    And staff me comfort still.
My table thou hast furnished
    In presence of my foes;
My head thou dost with oil anoint,
    And my cup overflows.
Goodness and mercy all my life
    Shall surely follow me:
And in God's house for evermore
    My dwelling-place shall be.

The Minister invited us to hear more comforting words from the scriptures; among those which he read were words of Jesus from the Gospel according to St John (Chapter 14 verses 1 to 6):

Jesus said to his disciples, 'Do not let your hearts be troubled. Trust in God still, and trust in me. There are many rooms in my Father's house; if there were not, I should have told you. I am going now to prepare a place for you, and after I have gone and prepared you a place, I shall return to take you with me; so that where I am you may be too. You know the way to the place where I am going.' Thomas said, 'Lord, we do not know where you are going, so how can we know the way?' Jesus said, 'I am the Way, the Truth and the Life. No one can come to the Father except through me.'

After these readings a short address was given in which the Minister reminded the mourners of how important the Christian faith had been to Mary White and how she had been well-loved in the community. 'In her home,' he said, 'there was always a kindly welcome for all and a cheerful, encouraging word. She was a wonderful friend and neighbour and it would be no exaggeration to say that she lived to serve others.

'We feel a deep sense of loss and we sorrow at her passing from us; yet it is for ourselves that we sorrow for we shall miss her. We do not sorrow for her, because our faith tells us that she is beyond suffering and the hand of tragedy can no longer touch her, for she is at home in the Father's house. So we lift up our hearts and know that our faith in Christ is not misplaced: he is the conqueror of death and has opened the gates to life eternal.'

After the address, the Minister read some of the words from one of the oldest hymns of the Christian Church known as 'Te Deum Laudamus' (which is simply the first few words of the hymn in its original Latin version). It is a hymn which, since about the fourth century, has expressed much that is important in the Christian faith:

Thou art the King of glory, O Christ:
Thou art the everlasting Son of the Father:
When Thou hadst overcome the sharpness of death:
Thou didst open the Kingdom of Heaven to all believers.
Thou sittest at the right hand of God:
In the glory of the Father.
We believe that Thou shalt come to be our Judge:
We therefore pray Thee, help Thy servants whom Thou hast redeemed with Thy precious blood.
Make them to be numbered with Thy saints
In glory everlasting.

Prayers followed in which we gave thanks for the life of Mary White and asked God to comfort and help those whose lives had been saddened by her death.

The final hymn was one which had been a special favourite of Mrs White:

In heavenly love abiding,
  No change my heart shall fear;
And safe is such confiding,
  For nothing changes here:
The storm may roar without me,
  My heart may low be laid;
But God is round about me,
  And can I be dismayed?

Wherever he may guide me,
  No want shall turn me back;
My Shepherd is beside me,
  And nothing can I lack.
His wisdom ever waketh,
  His sight is never dim:
He knows the way he taketh,
  And I will walk with him.

Green pastures are before me,
  Which yet I have not seen;
Bright skies will soon be o'er me,
  Where the dark clouds have been.
My hope I cannot measure:
  My path to life is free:
My Saviour has my treasure,
  And he will walk with me.

After the Benediction 'The grace of the Lord Jesus Christ, and the love of God, and the fellowship of the Holy Spirit, be with you all. Amen', we followed the coffin as it was carried out of the church.

## At the Grave

The term 'the committal' is often used of the service at the graveside. The coffin was carried from the hearse and laid down at the graveside. The mourners gathered round and the undertakers slowly lowered the coffin into the grave.

We listened as the Minister read some verses from the Bible:

'earth to earth, ashes to ashes . . .'

'Fear not, I am the first and the last, and the Living One; I died and behold, I am alive for evermore and I have the keys of death.'

'Death is swallowed up in victory. O death, where is thy victory? O death, where is thy sting? Thanks be to God who gives us the victory through our Lord Jesus Christ.'

The Minister looked down into the grave as he said:

'We have entrusted our sister, Mary White, to God's merciful keeping and we now commit her body to the ground, earth to earth, ashes to ashes, dust to dust: in sure and certain hope of the resurrection to eternal life through our Lord Jesus Christ, who died, was buried and rose again for us: to him be glory for ever and ever.'

As the words, 'earth to earth, ashes to ashes, dust to dust' were said, a handful of earth was thrown into the grave, which later would be completely filled in by an employee at the cemetery.

The Minister said a brief prayer, giving thanks for the life of Mary White and again asking for comfort for her family at this sad time. The graveside service ended as he said the words of the Benediction.

As the mourners left the graveside, many greeted Mr White and other members of the family. Mr White told us afterwards how the service had been a great comfort to him and how the presence of so many friends who had loved and respected his wife helped him at such a sad time.

## Cremation

Many Christians choose cremation as a way of disposing of the body, rather than burial. If the funeral is at a crematorium rather than a cemetery, the mourners follow the coffin into a quiet, peaceful little chapel. The design may vary from one crematorium to another, but in the one that we visited, the coffin is laid in an alcove at the front, while the Minister stands at a lectern or reading desk facing the mourners who are sitting in pews. The service is similar to that at the graveside, except that when it comes to the committal, the Minister says, 'We have entrusted our sister to God's mercifu

eeping and we now commit her body to
e cremated, ashes to ashes, dust to dust
. . .' As he says these words, in this
articular crematorium, a curtain quietly
loses, hiding the coffin from view.

After the mourners leave, it is then
laced in the cremator, behind the chapel.
ometimes, mourners ask for the ashes of
heir loved one, which may then be
uried in a grave several days later, or
cattered at a place particularly loved by
he person who has died; the majority
refer neither of these and the ashes are
imply scattered by crematorium staff in
he so-called 'Garden of Rest' – a beautiful
arden which surrounds the crematorium.

Since there is no grave on which flowers
an be placed at the time of the funeral,
hese are usually laid out in an area
ear the chapel so that mourners can
ook at the tributes to the person who
as died.

# Christian Beliefs about Death

he funeral service described in this
ection is not necessarily the way in
vhich every Christian funeral would be
onducted though the main parts of it
vould almost certainly be found in some
orm or other. In the same way, if
Christians were asked about their beliefs
oncerning death and another life after
his one, they might answer in different
vays, though there would be agreement
bout the most important aspects.

Most Christians believe that death is
ot the end but that there is another life
f some kind after this one. They would
upport this belief by reference to
tatements which are made in the Bible.
hey might, however, disagree about the
ature of that next life. Roman Catholics
usually believe that there is a state
vhich they call Purgatory, in which the
oul of the person is being purified ready

to enter Heaven. Other Christians think
of death as a long sleep until a time
when all the souls are resurrected; while
others believe that at death the good will
go to God in Heaven and the bad will go
to a place of punishment.

Most would agree that they do not
*know* what happens after death, but they
*believe* that because Jesus died on the
Cross and rose from the dead three days
later, death is not something of which
they should be afraid.

Christians regard a funeral not so
much as a ceremony in which they *do*
something for the person who has died,
or even in which they say goodbye to a
loved one, but as a ceremony in which
they remind themselves of their essential
beliefs and in which they become aware
that their faith in God will help them to
face the sorrow which the death of a
loved one has brought.

*Task 1*
Outline the main items which you think
are important parts of a Christian funeral
service. Give reasons why you think each
item is important. What do you see as
the main purpose of having such a
service?

*Task 2*
Look again at the hymns which were
sung in the funeral described in this
section: do you think these were
appropriate hymns for such an occasion?
Give reasons for your answer.

*Task 3*
What Christian beliefs about death can
you see reflected in the words of the
service which has been described?

*Task 4*
A Christian may choose either burial or
cremation: what do you think are the
advantages and disadvantages of each
method of disposing of the dead?

# 19

# Muslim

At the end of the month of fasting, Ramadan, Muslims celebrate a festival known as Eid-ul-Fitr. During the festival they have special meals, exchange greetings cards and gifts with their friends and visit the cemetery to say prayers at the graves of relatives who have died.

The Ahmed family, at this time, went to the grave of Abdul, Mr Ahmed's father, who had died only six months previously. They told us that even in the midst of the happy celebrations of the festival, Muslims should remember the temporary nature of life and the importance of living correctly in order to ensure eternal life with Allah after death.

Death may be the end of this present life, but, to the Muslim, it is by no means final; the Qur'an, the Muslim's holy book, speaks of a day of resurrection when everyone will be brought back to life and, if it is the will of Allah, be re-united with family and friends. This belief had strengthened and comforted the Ahmed family at the time of Adbul's death.

## At the Time of Death

Adbul Ahmed was in his eightieth year and had been ill for some time; as he neared death he spoke in Arabic the words of the **Kalimah**, the most important declaration in the Muslim faith, which expressed the belief by which Abdul had lived:

'La ilaha illallah
Muhammadu rasulullah'
(There is no God but Allah
(and) Muhammad is Allah's messenger)

This belief had given meaning and purpose to all that Abdul had done during his life and it was important to express it as he neared death. When he died, his family recited words from the Qur'an:

'We belong to Allah, and to him we shall return.'

So both Abdul and his family at the time of death gave expression to beliefs which lay at the heart of their faith.

Muslims believe that the body should be buried as soon as possible after death, so Abdul's eldest son contacted the undertaker and the funeral arrangements were made. The body was taken to the mosque, carefully washed according to a Muslim ritual which begins with the washing of those parts the Muslim washes before he prays; the body was then wrapped in a white garment and Abdul's head was turned so that it faced to the right. The coffin was then placed inside the metal container which you can see in the photograph. This lies in a room set aside for the purpose, below the main prayer hall. There is a ledge on which the coffin

is the custom among Muslims. An important part of the funeral was the offering of the funeral prayer, known as **Salat al Janazah,** in the mosque. Prayer on this occasion was rather different from the regular prayer rite which is followed in Muslim worship, since at the funeral prayer there is no bowing or prostration.

The prayer began with the words in Arabic:

'Allahu Akbar'
(God is the greatest)

This was followed by the recitation of the first chapter of the Qur'an:

'In the name of Allah, the Compassionate, the Merciful.
Praise be to Allah, Lord of the Creation,
The Compassionate, the Merciful, King of Judgement Day!
You alone we worship and to you alone we pray for help!
Guide us to the straight path,
The path of those whom you have favoured,
Not of those who have incurred your wrath,
Nor of those who have gone astray.'

Prayers at the funeral

ests so that the body lies with the head facing towards Mecca, the direction which Abdul and every other Muslim faced every day to offer prayers. The white garment in which Abdul was wrapped was the one which, some years earlier, he had worn when he made the pilgrimage to Mecca. All pilgrims are dressed alike to emphasise the idea that all are equal in the sight of Allah, and it is the custom if the dead person has made the pilgrimage to use this same garment as a shroud.

## The Funeral

Friends and relatives were informed of Abdul's death so that they could attend the funeral. Only male friends and members of the family attended, for this

119

The Imam talks to the mourners

## At the Cemetery

Relatives and friends carried the coffin to the hearse and the body was taken to the cemetery for burial. (Cremation is forbidden in Islam, so the body is always buried.)

In the local cemetery there is a section set aside for the Muslim community; this part looks very orderly, with all the gravestones of a similar size and shape and each grave marked out by a raised mound, since walking over a grave or sitting on one is regarded as disrespectful to the dead. Each grave lies in the direction of north-east to south-west and the memorial stone is at the south-west end. This is because the Muslim's body should be buried with the face towards Mecca.

Abdul Ahmed's coffin was lowered into the grave prepared for him, with the head at the south-west end; this meant that since his head was facing to the right, he was now facing in the direction of Mecca.

At the graveside, parts of the Qur'an were recited and prayers were said for Mr Ahmed before the mourners returned to the family home. Seven days later they returned to the grave and again offered prayers. There will be many occasions in the future when the family will visit the grave; on each occasion they say the words:

'Peace be upon you; may Allah forgive us all. You went to him before us and we will follow you.'

For a second time the Imam led the congregation in the words 'Allahu Akbar', followed by the words of a prayer known as Ibrahim's prayer. After a third 'Allahu Akbar' the men remained silent saying their own prayers for Abdul Ahmed. The fourth 'Allahu Akbar' was followed by the peace greetings which are a part of the regular Muslim prayers, 'Peace be upon you and the mercy of Allah.'

The congregation sat down on the floor and the Imam addressed them. In his address he reminded them of the words of Muhammad about those things of value which a faithful Muslim may leave behind him when he dies. A true Muslim like Abdul Ahmed leaves behind an example for his children to follow; he leaves behind his experience of life from which others can learn; he leaves behind such wealth as he had which will care for his family. The Imam also spoke of the mercy of Allah who rewards the faithful.

## Life after Death

The Ahmed family are comforted by their belief that they are only temporarily separated from Abdul and will be reunited with him when a Day of Judgement

120

comes. Abdul's son spoke with confidence of his belief in a future life and referred to the words of the Qur'an:

'On that day shall faces beam with light, looking towards their Lord.'

Muslims look forward to a physical resurrection, and this is why death is followed by burial and never by cremation. We were also told of other words in the Qur'an:

'Does man think we shall not reunite his bones together again? Indeed, we can remould his very fingers.'

Abdul's son told us that a man's behaviour on earth decides his future life, for after death the soul will be required to answer questions put by angels about conduct during one's earthly life. A true believer, we were told, will exist in peace and happiness until the Day of Judgement; the unbeliever will be punished because the Prophets have shown him the way of obedience, peace and happiness but he has chosen to ignore their words.

On this last day, Allah will raise everyone and all will have to account for the way they have lived; the worthy will enter Paradise and the rest will suffer misery and despair. The Qur'an presents a picture in words which compares these two opposite states:

'On that day there shall be radiant faces of men well-pleased with their labours in a lofty garden. A gushing fountain shall be there and raised soft couches with goblets placed before them, silken cushions ranged in order and carpets richly spread.'
'On that day there will be downcast faces of men broken and worn out, burnt by a scorching fire, drinking from a seething fountain; their only food shall be bitter thorns which will neither sustain them nor satisfy their hunger.'

According to Muslim beliefs therefore, everyone is responsible for his ultimate destiny but if one is a true believer and asks for forgiveness for his misdeeds, the Muslim is confident that Allah will be merciful.

*Task 1*
(a) What particular difficulties have to be faced by Muslims living in a non-Muslim country as far as death is concerned?
(b) Imagine you are a Muslim who has recently moved into an area of Britain where there are no facilities provided for Muslim funerals. Write a letter to the local authority explaining what is needed and asking for help.

*Task 2*
What beliefs about Allah held by Muslims are reflected in the customs associated with death?

*Task 3*
What three things had Abdul Ahmed left behind, according to the Imam? How valuable do you regard these to be? What others could you add to the list which you hope could be said about your life?

*Task 4*
Write a description of the Muslim beliefs about Heaven and Hell, or, if you prefer, draw pictures to illustrate these.

*Task 5*
Many Muslims talk about good and bad deeds being weighed against each other on Judgement Day. Describe deeds which you think might be placed on the 'good side' of the balance.

# 20
# Sikh

A leading member of the Sikh community has died. On the day of the funeral, his coffin was carried from the gurdwara to the waiting hearse for its final journey to the crematorium.

Naturally, the death has brought great sadness to the community as a whole, but they have taken comfort from the words of the Guru Granth Sahib, the Sikh holy book. It is also customary among Sikhs to sing hymns in times of sorrow; even if news of a death in India reaches a Sikh family in Britain, appropriate hymns may be sung in the home. One of the hymns of the Gurus which is often used at such a time of grief is that written by Guru Arjan who was the fifth leader of the Sikh faith.

Leaving the gurdwara

Let your heart sing praises of the Formless
One;
This should be your righteous course.
Keep your tongue pure by the touch of His
name,
It will give you peace of mind.
With your eyes, behold the splendour of
God's presence.
The company of the faithful will banish
every other presence from your sight.
Walk in the way of God;
With every step you take you will be
treading down evil inclinations.
With your hands do God's work and with
your ears listen to His instruction.

## At the Time of Death

The death took place in hospital and
arrangements were made by the family
for the funeral. The body was removed to
the undertaker's chapel of rest. Here the
undertaker allowed the sons of the family
to carry out certain duties which Sikhs
believe are important. The sons brought
yoghurt which was mixed with water and
this was used to wash the body. Sikhs
consider yoghurt to be an important
purifying substance.

When the washing was complete, the
body was clothed in a completely new
outfit, even the shoes were unused. They
were particularly careful to include the
important symbols of the Sikh faith
which are mentioned on page 64:

*Kaachs* – the shorts
*Kanga* – the comb
*Kara* – the bracelet
*Kirpan* – the sword.

Once they had carried out these duties,
they placed the body of their father in
the coffin.

## The Funeral

Sikhs practise cremation, so the funeral
took place at the local crematorium.

Earlier on the day of the funeral, however,
the coffin was taken from the chapel of
rest to the family home. Many friends
and relatives came to file past the open
coffin, taking a last look at their friend
who had died. Some even spoke to the
body and others openly expressed their
grief. Such customs are important to
Sikhs as a way of coming to terms with
the fact that their loved one really has
died. They believe that it is helpful for
sorrow to be expressed rather than hidden
inside.

Later that morning, after prayers had
been said for the soul of the dead man,
the coffin was taken from the home to
the gurdwara, the Sikh temple. Here
again the coffin lid was removed so that
other members of the Sikh community
could pay their last respects to their
friend who had played a leading part in
many matters affecting the whole Sikh
community.

When it was time to leave for the
crematorium, the lid was finally placed
on the coffin and the funeral procession
moved off from the gurdwara. Crowds of
friends and relatives followed the hearse
in which there were so many floral
tributes that some had to be carried on
the roof.

At the crematorium

On arrival at the crematorium, the mourners followed the coffin into the chapel for a brief service. The coffin was placed in an alcove at the front, in the view of all the congregation. The service consisted of the recitation of a prayer known as the **Sohila**, the Sikh evening prayer which Sikhs generally use at the end of each day. This recitation of the prayer was led by the Granthi from the gurdwara. Part of the prayer is:

'Know the real purpose of being here and gather up your treasure under the guidance of the true Guru. Make your mind God's home. If he abides with you undisturbed, you will not be reborn.'

After this prayer the eldest son of the family pressed a button which operates the mechanism to draw curtains across the alcove hiding the coffin from view. If this death had occurred in India, it is likely that the body would have been burned on an open funeral pyre similar to that described in the chapter on death in Hinduism. The eldest son would have been responsible for lighting such a funeral pyre.

When the curtains had been drawn across the alcove, the mourners quietly filed out of the crematorium. There was, however, one more task to be performed by the sons: they had arranged previously with the crematorium authorities that they would be present when the coffin was placed in the cremator. As their final act for their dead father, each son touched the coffin as it slid into the cremator.

## At the Gurdwara

The mourners returned to the gurdwara where they listened to readings from the

Guru Granth Sahib and recited prayers. Some men stood up and paid tribute to their friend who had died, saying that he had been a true Sikh and a good friend.

The service ended with the prayer known as the **Ardas** which is used in all Sikh worship; also everyone shared in the sweet food, **Karah Parshad**, which is another regular feature of Sikh worship. On this occasion, however, besides indicating the view that all present are equal, many Sikhs say it is a reminder that the normal activities of life must go on even although a loved one has died.

A copy of the holy book had been placed carefully in one room of the family home and during the ten days following the funeral it was read from beginning to end by a succession of readers. During this time friends called at the home, listened to part of the reading and offered their sympathy to the family.

# Beliefs about Death

We talked with a member of the Sikh community, Mr Ajit Singh, about the Sikh customs and beliefs relating to death.

*Our question:* What beliefs do Sikhs hold about life after death?

*Answer:* We believe in the rebirth or reincarnation of the soul according to the **Karma** we have built up; by this I mean that the soul will be born again depending on how the person's life has been lived.

*Our question:* Hindus also believe in Karma and reincarnation; is there any difference between what you believe about this and what Hindus believe?

*Answer:* I think the main difference lies in the fact that Sikhs believe that **Mukti**, i.e. liberation from being reborn, comes through the grace of God. A Sikh must become 'gurmukh' or 'God-filled' if he wishes to avoid being reborn. This is to be achieved by listening to the words of the Gurus, meditating on the Name of God and offering worship in the presence of the **Sangat,** i.e. the congregation of Sikhs. We believe the words of the Gurus who tell us that in the company of good people one learns goodness. If a man or a woman makes a sincere attempt to find God through these ways, then God in his love and grace will grant the believer release from the cycle of death and rebirth and the soul will be with God. This is what the words of the **Sohila** mean, which we recited at the funeral, 'If he abides with you undisturbed, you will not be reborn.'

*Our question:* How different is the funeral we have witnessed from a funeral in a Sikh community in India?

*Answer:* In India, the body would have been carried from the home to a place outside the village, while hymns were sung. A funeral pyre would have been built up and the body placed on it. The eldest son would have lit the fire and we would have seen the body being burned. Since we cannot do that in Britain, we follow the pattern of funeral which you have seen, but our essential customs are still being observed in accordance with our beliefs.

*Our question:* It is often the custom for a monument or a memorial stone to be erected, especially for someone well-known and well-loved in the community. Will this be done for your friend who has died?

*Answer:* No! Sikhs do not believe that they should have such monuments. The ashes will be collected from the crematorium and will be thrown into a river by the close relatives who will not even look back once they have done this. Sikhs are taught that they must remember the words of our holy book:

'The dawn of a new day is the herald of a sunset. Earth is not our permanent home.'

## Task 1

(a) What are the duties of the eldest son in a Sikh family when a parent has died?

(b) What is there in the Sikh customs which helps the mourners come to terms with the death of their loved one?

(c) In what ways is respect for the person who has died shown in the Sikh funeral customs?

## Task 2

Do you agree with the Sikh view that there should be no monuments for those who have died? What arguments would you present either for or against this view?

## Task 3

List the ways in which, according to Sikh teaching, a person can become 'Mukti', i.e. released from rebirth.

## Task 4

Consider the following words of Guru Nanak which are part of the Japji, an important section of the Guru Granth Sahib:

'We do not become saints or sinners by merely saying that we are:
It is the actions that are recorded.
According to the seed we sow, is the fruit we reap.
By God's grace, O Nanak, man must either be saved or transmigrate.' (i.e. be reborn)

(a) Express in your own words the idea contained in that passage and also the advice given in the prayer known as the Sohila quoted on page 124.

(b) What do you consider to be the purpose of 'being here'?

# Additional Tasks on Death

1 Consider how death is presented in a variety of television programmes. How can you tell, for example, in a film that someone has died even before that fact is mentioned, or in a news programme that the newscaster is about to mention that someone has died? What conclusions can you draw from such observations?

2 When many people talk about a death they often avoid the actual word and use expressions like, 'passed away' or 'gone to rest'. Make a list of other similar expressions used about death. Why do you think people use such expressions instead of saying, 'he is dead'?

3 Most religions teach that there is another life of some kind after this one. Attempt to sort out your own beliefs about this by either a class discussion or by individual writing. Remember, it is not enough to say *what* you believe; also say *why* you think it is a valid belief to hold.

4 If most religions teach that there is another life after this one, why does death produce so much sadness, even in very religious people? In what ways do you think a religious faith can help a person face the death of a loved one?

5 In many faiths, gravestones are erected in memory of the person who has died. What are your views about this? Are there other, and perhaps better ways of honouring and remembering the loved one who has died?

6 There are fewer photographs in the chapters about death in this book than in the other sections. Why do you think it is more difficult to obtain photographs relating to death?

# General Tasks

The following suggested tasks give you an opportunity at the end of this study to review some of the ideas which you have thought about during the course.

1. Many people of different faiths, though they do not show much commitment at other times, turn to their religion for a ceremony for birth, marriage and death. Why do you think this is so?

2. In some faiths, if you have not been through one of the earlier ceremonies, you may not be permitted to have one of those which come later: e.g. in some Christian Churches, if you have not been baptised, either as a baby or since then, you may not be allowed to marry within that Church. Discuss reasons why you think this is the case. Do you agree or disagree with this view? Give reasons for your answer.

3. Religious Education is said to be concerned with questions of meaning, purpose and values. What questions about meaning, purpose and values have been raised for you by the course you have just completed? What answers, if any, have you found?

4. Why do you think all religions have ceremonies relating to birth, marriage and death? In what way are these events concerned with a search for meaning and purpose in life?

5. (a) Which of the ceremonies you have studied in this course has most impressed you? Give reasons for your answer.
   (b) If this ceremony is not in the faith which you follow yourself, do you think the important parts of it could be used in your faith, without conflicting with the basic beliefs of your faith? In what way would this improve, in your opinion, the ceremony for the same event in your faith?

# Index